Ono Ono Girl's Hula

*Carolyn Lei-lanilau*

# Ono Ono
# Girl's Hula

*The University of Wisconsin Press*

The University of Wisconsin Press
2537 Daniels Street
Madison, Wisconsin 53718

3 Henrietta Street
London WC2E 8LU, England

Earlier versions of some of the chapters in this book appeared in the following publications: "The Presence of Lite Spam," "'*Aumakua*: An Example of Hawaiian Thought Processes," and "From Latin to Latino; from *Nopales* to *Panini*," in *Making More Waves*, Beacon Press, 1997; "*Almost* a Man," in *(Re)mapping the Occident*, University of California Press, 1995; "From the Diary of *Bu Yau Shu Cai*," in *Yellow Silk* 12.4; "Craig the Early Beat Influence" and "The Cosmogony of the Pineapple Cannery," in *Bamboo Ridge* 60; "Vision 2" and "Mona Lisa Grandma," in *Blue Mesa* 6; "How Chicano Philosophy Influenced Counter-Revolutionary Lau's Educating Immigrant Asians et al.," in *The Raven Chronicles* 3.3; Selections from *Ono Ono Girl's Hula*, in ZYZZYVA 8.2.

Library of Congress Cataloging-in-Publication Data
Lei-lanilau, Carolyn.
    Ono Ono girl's hula / Carolyn Lei-lanilau.
    196 pp.        cm.
    ISBN 0-299-15630-3 (cloth: alk. paper).   ISBN 0-299-15634-6 (pbk.: alk. paper).
    1. Lei-lanilau, Carolyn.   2. Chinese Americans—Hawaii—Biography.   3. Chinese Americans—Hawaii—Ethnic identity.   4. Hawaii—Biography.
    I. Title.
    E184.C5L55        1997
    996.9'004951—dc21        97-7216

for

Jacqueline Lokelani

What a teacher!

*Some* sister

# CONTENTS

# CHAPTER 2
# Parthenogenesis                                                        78

## CHAPTER 6
### Ho'okolohe, heh heh

**177**

# M A H A L O

*Acknowledgments*

Thank you Bill Blake for all your translated voices stirring my waking and sleeping.

Thank you to Samuel Beckett whose *adagio* is the incantation of prayer.

*Merci beaucoup beaucoup beaucoup a Professor Pierre LeBlewett! Gloria in excelsis Saint Peter!* Thank you for believing in me for no reason. Thanks for cajoling me into believing that I could write wisdom, orgasm, jokes, and tricks into philosophy our bedrock. Thenkyew Pamela Fletcher for ya red earth brains (that's Hawaiian honey!) "*Dziekuje!*"

During the first days of my writing career, I was privileged to have been inspired by the writers Jack Gilbert and Stan Rice, Stan Rice and Jack Gilbert. Thank you Stan for the many many pages of pencil and single-spaced typed criticism—the "shit-detector needle"—which would demand that logic and lyric match creation. Jack, thank you for the many years of shepherding me and my young daughters in the nature(s) and production(s) of vision. Having practiced your instructions this lifetime, we hope we now know what it means to benefit from "the normal excellence of long accomplishment."

A most humble *gratia* to Robin T. Lakoff, who took time from her very busy schedule to read and support this book, which I hope will inspire new commands in linguistics. Thank you to my friend, writer, and native sister, Ramona Wilson, who also read and supported the work. Thank you to Rosalie M. Robertson, the best editor a writer could dare to imagine!

*Xie xie*, thank you, to the semiotician Zhao Yi Heng, Henry Zhao, and the scholar Zhang Ziqing. A humble bow at the honorable gate of my Chinese language teacher, Ni Tai Tai, Frances Nivolo, who encouraged me with insightful pep talks and inspired me to explore Chinese further.

*Mahalo nui loa*, my warmest *aloha* to Maile Meyer at Native Books. It was Maile who early on informed me about the changing nature of *mana'o ho'o kūkū*, Hawaiian metaphors.

Thank you to Howard Junker and ZYZZYVA for publishing the first essay; and also *Bamboo Ridge, Blue Mesa, Yellow Silk, Raven Chronicles*. Thanks to my Faithful Corrector, neighbor Anne Irving, who scrutinized And understood my English when I wanted it to be.

*Mahalo* to *kanaka wahine*, a Hawaiian woman who shared her *mana* with me, *kumu hula* Naomi Leina'la Kalama. *Mahalo* to your sacred ears who knew what I was trying to say or ask. *Mahalo* to your loving tongue(s) and hands that danced or wrote your *mana'o* with me, eager to gather shards, threads, the *pili* grass to breathe, compress, thatch our fragile Hawaiian values into how a *kanaka* might express herself.

*Mahalo* to Aunty Kika who named *Ono Ono* Girl at Earl's *lū'au*. *Mahalo* to Aunty Bea who took me into her California *ahupua'a* while adapting *mele* from Hawai'i to enjoy *mana* in the fields, watercress, streams, wild fig trees, frogs and crickets, the abandoned stone houses built by the Chinese during the Gold Rush. O to see Aunty Bea transformed into a young deer in her jeans and T-shirt as she praised the land in simple talk! *Mahalo* to my Kaleponi *'ohana*.

Thank you Janis Joplin and Kekuhi Kanahele for your powerful *hā* and to Milton Murayama for sharing laughs and secrets. Thank you to Rob Wilson whatever time zone you're in and to Candice Fujikane, who suggested a chapter on my genealogy. *Mahalo* to the great writer Gary Pak for visionary insights. A long haul from undergraduate days until now—thank you pal, thank you Morgan Blair aka Faye Kicknosway. An *ono* thanks to my West O'ahu officemate, Dr. Linda Nishigaya and to all the nice nice folks at the UH Mānoa—especially Summer Session. Thank you, Diane Mark, Malia Pangilinan, Kimiko Hahn, Victor Hernandez Cruz, Leialoha Perkins, Nancy Nordhoff (Cottages at Hedgebrook in Washington) and The California Arts Council.

*Merci beaucoup* to my handsome friend, the intelligent writer/editor, Thomas Avena, who has been forever good to me. *Merci aussi* to our son, the maverick writer/editor, Bryan Malessa.

Thank you to George Kitahara Kich for being such a good brother. Wild applause to Victor Anderson and Frank Shawl from the Shawl-Anderson Dance Center: Victor got me addicted to *adagio* in the precise walk and Frank taught me how to pretzel. *Arigato* to the best ballet teacher Carolyn Goto who corrected and encouraged me with the best metaphors. "Fill the space with your shape!" she exclaimed.

Thank you to my girlfriends, Renee Swayne, Sophia H., Lisa Wong, Diane Troy, Julie Chan, Harriet Gulassa, Tobey Kaplan, and Jean Ready Froning. Pinches to my Portagee sweetie, Steve, at Bridgeway. And how about the sexiest, smartest, fun-loving *chic* chick down-home nice-gracious—the one and only Elaine Kim in Dior or sweats?

A teacher is no one without students and here's my list of RAVORITES: Carrie Takahata, Chip Nakagawa, Carolyn Uehara, and Miss California, Mimi Pham. And thank you to my colleagues the Evergreen posse Ernestine Kimbro, Justino Balderama, and Therese Saliba. Irene Estrella no longer smokes; Maydene Young, *no ka oi*! Thank you Laura, thank you Les Honda, and Kennrick Yoshida.

*Auē! kala mai ia'u*: yikes! Everyone who knows my work is aware how bored I am with the T'ang. However, there are hundreds of thousands of Chinese writers whom I love: thank you to the great Chinese writers Lu Xun, who has inspired me since 1980 when I first began my affair with China; Qiu Jin, Ba Qin, Feng Jicai, Nu Shu sisters and Zhang Jie—*xie, xie*.

Finally, thank you to my girls Eirelan Kai'ipo and Kalea-Qyana who endure, argue, and love me throughout EVerything. Thank you to my Chinese cousins who babysat and loved me and scolded and supported me all my years on this earth—to Nana, Beatie, and Flossie: Nelia Lee, Beatrice Lee Higuchi, and Florence Lee Wong. *Mahalo* to Emela, Rosemarie, Annette, Uncle Walter, and the rest of my Hawaiian *'ohana* that I am finally meeting and will be meeting. *Xie xie* to Xu Tao aka Steven Thomas, Steve Xu, who brought me to and through many adventures.

*Mahalo* to my perfect and still-teaching-me mother Mildred Chong Lau; to my daddy, my father John Winfred/Winfield, and my sister Jacqueline Lokelani whom I miss and for whom this book was written. *Mahalo*

## *O L I*

The *oli* is a chant, an epiphany or ejaculation. *ONO ONO GIRL'S HULA* is a *lei*, a collection of chants which *haku*, weave, from within the author's physical and spiritual being. As a child, the author was raised by her maternal eldest aunt who spoke to her exclusively in the Chinese Hakka dialect. However, due to the stigma attached to belonging to the class of "big feet, independent and aggressive women," as well as personal experiences that reflected this contempt, the author rarely acknowledged her mother's ancestry. Her older sister nonetheless verbally expressed pride in being Hakka. Not only that, Jacqueline Lokelani was a student of the legendary *kumu hula* ʻIolani Luahine, who was considered a witch at that time.

When the author grew up in Hawaiʻi, there were no ESL classes, there was only English Standard school and although she is Hawaiian, there was tremendous pressure from within and without not to speak or be Hawaiian. Her father conversed in Hawaiian only outside the house in the yard when Hawaiian-speaking relatives or friends would visit. English, according to the first pronunciation in the dictionary, was spoken in the home. Her father tested her on Word Wealth each week; her mother, on spelling and grammar: proudly, the family was a home without accent. While among English speakers this may seem traumatic, this norm was merely the "plate lunch syndrome" upon which many of the households in Hawaiʻi operated; and although the author was not permitted to converse in Hawaiian, it was impossible not to say *pūneʻe, lānai, kau kau, poi, mahalo, aloha, haole, pau hana, pilau, pohō, kuleana, pala niho, kūkae, kāpulu, kapu, kapakahi, manini, momona, pilikia, papaʻa* instead of couch, veranda, eat, a pudding made from taro, thank you, hello/love, white person, done work, rotten, loss, responsibility, leftovers, shit, slipshod, taboo, crooked, stingy, fat, trouble, burnt. These were the everyday words, and there were also the place names: Waikīkī, Waimanalo, Honolulu, Hanauma Bay, the *pali*, Nuʻuanu. These sounds and images were/are in the air, waters, heat, the red volcanic dirt: *'āina*. What a confusing time it was for the author when she heard the Hawaiian language but was *kapu*, forbidden, to "speak" or be Hawaiian!

Eventually, the author found herself in high school studying Latin and French. When the taste of accent was formally introduced to her, she loved it. Years later, the Beijing and Tianjin accents were incorporated into her speech, available to her when she studied Chinese. In 1987, the Hawaiian language was voted by the Hawai'i legislature to be an official language. By then, the author had accomplished her interests in medieval Chinese literature and philosophy and was bored. Meanwhile the 1974 Kalama Valley, Waiāhole/Waikāne and Kaho'olawe land struggles had sparked the current sovereignty movement in Hawai'i. In 1993, as she curated an event at the Oakland Museum in honor of the one-hundredth anniversary commemorating the overthrow of Lili'uokalani (the last Hawaiian monarch), the author realized that finally, it was safe to be *kanaka*.

Hence, these essays represent the metaphors of many languages in and on the author's tongue and hands. Originally, the title of this book was *Maloko o Ka Pu'uwai o Laka*, which means *Within Laka's Heart*. Who is Laka? Laka is the male deity of the forest and the female deity of the *hula*. When writing these essays, the author set out to perform a task: to be *pono*. In the name of Laka, the author wrote her *mana'o*, her opinions, which she hoped would honor, humor, please the deity. In the birth of this book, the icon ONO ONO GIRL revealed herself; hence, the title was transformed to be ONO ONO GIRL'S HULA and the correct spelling of " *'ono*" was changed to reflect common usage. On his album *E Ala Ē*, Israel Kamakawiwo'ole refers to "Hawaiians like us" and he is corrected "like, 'you.'" And Iz continues, "Hard to find, eh?" The "we Hawaiians" expressed in the text refers to Hawaiians imperfect and wonderful; past, present, or future; who are like and unlike, who might share and also disagree with the author. As the languages, ideas, and concepts expressed, revealed, and explored in these essays spring from the author's body, they may *seem* new and perhaps confusing to the reader; therefore, the author repeats the ideas in various circumstances like a refrain to *ha 'ina mai ana ka pu ana*, "to tell the story," that is, to really tell the story in the full spirit of *aloha*.

Ono Ono Girl's Hula

# 1

# Illegible Handwriting

English, the Foreign Body
on the *Piko* of *Keiki o Ka ʻĀina*

## *Lūʻau* (the banquet, psyche)

**Epiphanies:** Friday Night Poker Game

**Vision 2:** Algebra and Latin Replacing Math and Gambling

**Ejaculations:** No Neck, Flat Nose; Has Classic Eyebrows: HCCA (The Hawaii Chinese Civic Association), Junior Chapter

**Vision 4:** My Sweet *ʻŌkole* or *Manaʻo* vs. *Maneʻo*

**Vision 5:** Inside Outside as a Chinese *Wahine*

**Euphoria:** Elevated to "Aunty"

### Epiphanies
Sweet Lei-lani, Sweet Girl, *Ono*
Banquet on Thumper (my pet rabbit)
Hawaiʻi against the barbarians: Catholic by day; Pagan, rest of the time
Grandma, the beauty; my otherside cousin Miss Hawaiʻi and Aunty Spam

**Vision 2**
Writing and Drawing during punishment time
No interest in arithmetic    Stabbing my leather volleyball
                             Swinging in the *lichee* tree; the orchids and *Tai Yi*
                             Stanley and the moon    The slop man and the fig tree
                                   My first play and stories based on tampax ads

                             **Ejaculations**
                             My two mothers—especially the hood ornament
                             Cherries: drinking mercury; eating cherry chili
                             peppers
Showing our parts behind the chair
Norman Cow: Yellow *American* vs. Fu Wen and the Taiwan opera

**Vision 4:** My *ʻŌkole*
How to get boyfren
Learning to drive without instruction
Surviving private education and real life as artist
The Mainland vs. *Ala Moana*

**Vision 5: The Adventures of** *ONO ONO* **GIRL**
HPD: living legends of the archetype warrior class

                             **Euphoria**
                             The sixties and my 34D bra
             No Longa Chinese; Portagee/Hawaiian: no Eurasia
                       lawyers: lying and the hunt
Xu Tao, my (sometimes) Greatest Love

# Author's Note

All my life, someone was reminding me how *lōlō* (stupid) I was. At the same time, some nagging angel suggested that at least my own ideas were interesting. I have read a lot of books and studied a number of languages. I put my psyche in what I'll call Upside Down just so I could **understand** life. Now that I have had one or two things published and "other" Chinese Americans are making loads of money writing fiction, the hopeful phone calls and letters from my

literati relatives in Hawai'i and China urge me to join ranks with the Chinese American fiction set: "Dolling, why don't you write fiction and make oodles and oodles of money? Poetry is *so hard.*" And my husband, who knows what no good I'm always up to, shakes his head in agreement: "Philosophy's a deadend. Nobody will buy it."
—How can I tell my closest people that I am dysfunctional, cannot write in vertical columns? Has anyone ever lived chapter 2 ever following chapter 1 in everyday get-up-and-make-the-coffee real life? A friend who is a therapist calmly informed me that life is not the way the self-help books describe. (You should see the self-help book booths at the American Booksellers Convention!) I asked why these books are written if life never reflects what the books outline? And he says, "because they're *just books.*"

When I was in college and feeling depressed because I thought Rilke had written it All, Jack Gilbert confided that "No, Carolyn, the books never tell you about real life." So, I'm writing these thoughts no differently from my other books. As introduction, I'd just like to mention that I am aware my nonfiction/poetry/prose/history/traditional folk artsy does not read like my idol Julia Kristeva (mine is more silly) or some sort of elevated book report. I just believe that readers—livers of life—Can relate to the complexity of life directly through my text (dangling preps; single subjects, plural verbs; past & present tensely harmonic). I don't believe it matters that I grew up in a territory, fragmented by my parents' own insecurities about Hawai'i as a colony of the mainland. Why?

because, I'm a genius: I believe Blake. Yes, I did work for Perls and was under the spell of Gestaltvision; and yes, my whole being is a sort of particle operating in medieval and contemporary metaphysics. Because we are *something*—we all—are male and female. Spiritual, hungry. We output in formal orderly packages and cannot live with natural chaos. So, some people drive Saabs and have face-lifts. Others have guns. That existing, isn't it about time that a citizen could deserve more from entertaining literature than mere patina? For you who like philosophy, believe it or not, I began with the Germans and was finished off by the Chinese. For those who *imagine* that you cannot understand philosophy, if you can tap your head and rub your tummy; if you can IBM and Macintosh; if you ever held two jobs, my way of writing is just a kind of conscious impression of—of multiculturalism! I wanted me, a woman, to write a book of philosophy based on "assorted data." "Why can't this be done?" I posed (then worried). Why don't women write books on philosophy? (See my "Notes on Philosophy," written as response to

Professor Wing-Tsit Chan's comments during the 500th Anniversary of Kung Fuzi's birth).

Voluntarily, I write this book because this *idea* is way behind schedule on the publication ladder—while the hopeful calls from my cousins still come.

## Introduction or All of Epiphanies

Gin and chocolates time: slide-show time. This is a sort of shadowy puppet play where you are expected to snooze.—I might be writing in English but my efforts have never been to please the pleased-with-self client. While lots of folks like to eat Chinese food from boxes and maybe have even seen an "about Chinese" movie, in all probability, you were privy to whitewashed Chinese Americana. What I mean is that the average American Chinaphile is so sheltered about Chinese. Take me, for instance, I grew up "basically Chinese." Though my father is motley Chinese, I am mostly gypsy-gened Hakka. While the Chinese around me were influenced by the Hawaiians—a complete system in and of itself—my orientation was primarily *bourgeois*. At one time, I could speak French better and could translate Latin but dared not utter *ching* or *chong* or *ling* or *tong*. Did not want to yell that loud grease-talk. As a kid, I saw one or two movies. Had the classic Pearl Buck grandmother book read to me. I had seen Taiwan-Mandarin and Cantonese, but more European operas. Only when I had my kids—that's when I began to groove in Chinese. I forced my older daughter Eirelan to study characters on Saturdays instead of allowing her to join Bluebirds. After Ana was born, I lied. I told Mrs. Lee that Ana was six when she was still four just so she and Eirelan who was nine could have the "joy" of studying together. I studied Mandarin. I pushed away my friends and family for about ten years just so I could start from the beginning and maybe end up as an old lady satisfied that I had read all the literature, philosophy, and history written by Chinese. I was insane. During that time, I went to China twice to study and work. I only had Chinese from China boyfriends. And, I was selective: they had to have titles and exotic occupations like "paleontologist" or "semiotician." My daughters hated me. Then, by accident, I met my husband. The one place that I vowed never to go to he's from: Xi'an. You know the story of the ballerina and the tin soldier? He's the stone soldier. The point is that the ballerina did not know military life and the soldier never knew *sa-lon*.

We are good only at fucking and fighting: talk about being exactly alike in temperament. I am living the intertextual real stuff—the nonfiction about my "feeling" Chinese, Hawaiian, American. Those "other" Asian American accounts are so removed and outdated. And also, no mo guts, their kind talk: full stomach of descriptive talk, the veneer. I learned to climb trees without shoes.
Never got into those stylized Asian American motifs.

—Fer gawds sakes don't ask me if I'm Amy or Maxine. They are sane; I am SHAMeless.

## The CreaTion Myth of *ONO ONO* GIRL

This crusade begins in Hawai'i. Not the Hawai'i with condos and shopping malls. No, that is not Hawai'i. The Hawai'i that most people know is some mutant demon of which Pele is demanding due respect. When I grew up in Honolulu, nobody ever saw a real eruption except people on the Big Island. Pele was happy: No active volcanoes! We had dull happy lives in our grass shacks. We all lived in dried grass mansions. Naked, mostly, we mumbled and grunted. We lived on seaweed, shark's fins, and swung on vines. Life was Slow. The air was still and always quiet. Distinctly, I remember reading MOBY DICK and wondering why sexual instinct had not yet revealed themselves in my adolescent blossoming. I looked out my bedroom window. There was the hung wash. Eventually, my mother and I would leave to visit my bedridden grandma. My room was neatly in order. Nothing in or outside the room was misplaced and it had to do with the stillness or air that moved in the territorial frame. Innocence. Island mentality. Provincial upbringing. All I knew was private school in the day, speaking good English at home after. As an example: nobody spoke pidgin in my father's house. Nobody spoke Chinese. If you said a word in English, it was *de rigueur* to employ the first pronunciation because my mother always trailed with Correct on her hard drive. If you mispronounced a word, she nailed you. When my father's relatives showed up from Australia—talk about fun. And picking up accent! But as far as "correct speech" was concerned, nothing but logic and diagrams were acceptable to the family. Imagine how stunned I was when I transferred to a girls' high school and overheard "fuck" spoken—quite correctly, with the hormones and discontent towards authority active. I guess I was "sheltered." I was fascinated that these lovely *hula*, island, girls swishing in their pleated skirts; lips reflecting torch gingers, plumerias, and respectfully bred hibiscus, forming the "f" like a cannon loading and then burning the smooth saintly air with the explosive "uck," "fuck" word. Though nominally registered, this piece was yet another factor in my footnotes on "I hear. I see. I think; therefore, so what?"

## *ONO ONO* GIRL'S Actual Contemporary Birth

Ever since I saw and heard the word *homunculus*, that little kewpie has reappeared as the Good Angel, My Muse, Little Lulu, William Blake, my male teachers, and/or students. The thrill with imagination and artists is that you never know *what* we're "imagining" "believing" "thinking." Not that the non-artist is excluded from being an artist. As a matter of fact, there are armies of non-artists calling themselves "artist." I don't think the artist goes around visibly impressed with her torments of living with the lights on day and night day after day, year after year. Imagine the utility bill? He is too "sensitive" "fragile" and may even appear "depressed" while centered deep in that meditative clear. Worst, if the visions carried by her Are (theoretically universal and correct) revolutionary, demanding and challenging to television, or harder to digest than Thai food, what choice except for him to feel painfully, tragically, shy? All work must be produced in isolation. It is this solitude, this peace, this privacy that provides beatific feast where monsieur homunculus sez what.

**Thass the problem with man-kine English words and ideas. At her moment of birth *ONO ONO* GIRL wass free because when was born in the middle of song between two aunties; one spiritual, the other *kolohe*.** *ONO ONO* GIRL was non-not(h)ing until she was dancing *hula* at Earl and Clifford's *lū'au*—can you believe *ONO ONO* GIRL wass born in a garage in Modesto! Oh, she made all kine mistakes and could read Yolanda's mind as *ONO ONO* GIRL wass making hand and feet mistakes but *ONO ONO* GIRL kept on smiiling and smiiling and shaking dose hips dancing and dancing. And *ONO ONO* GIRL was **being born**: she was no longer No-nahting. Her dance of mistakes was her *pule*, her prayer, and she got two fat-fat kisses from Aunty Bea and Aunty Kika when the music was *pau* and she got two warm sweet hugs from the universes Aunty Kika and Aunty Bea and the *'ohana*, sista, aunty, *tūtū* still with all her own teeth: the institution was with *ONO ONO* GIRL. *Maika'i no!*

## *Papa* and *Wākea* Post Annexation and Statehood

The gods in the one temple were Mildred Chong and John Winfield Lau. At my other house, it was Tai Yi and five older cousins. Chez parents was like ballet class: with each spoken word, corresponded a physical act. My mother's favorite terms were, "That is Cor-rect!" or "that is In-correct!" Over the years, I have often retold the same old sortie how my father never uttered a sentence to me after he mourned that fact that "If you were a boy, I could take you to the baseball game." Daddy was god. Orderly, beautiful script. Made money. Secretive. My father was a statue, a portrait of a flag. Like all the aristocrat Hawaiians of the time, he was Republican and probably much more than the guy who went to 8:00 am mass every Sunday. He rarely drank and once in a great while he played his *ukulele* and sang Hawaiian songs. Poor Daddy, so so hard to be Hawaiian in his days. Impossible. So poor Daddy had to be Chinese instead except when he talked to his orchids or said "*Pehea oe?*" "Howzit?" when his friends came by. The sound of his "*Maika'i*" ("Great!") droplet of sound: *nahe nahe*, the Precious, I hold onto in rebuilding my *ahupua'a*, my every thing. It means so much to Hawaiians for our bodies to repeat the feelings and sounds of our ancestors that were nearly destroyed by missionaries and then tourists. We have a deep wound in our psyche that may take generations to heal and it can not be accomplished with the tool that we were taught to use, English.

Mother is so smart, it is not fair to have a mother that smart, that loving, that funny, and that determined to make her time on earth full of accomplishment. I can't be around her too much because her spirit and physical life take up nations of space. Still, she's my mother, and finally, at eighty-eight, she is slowing down to remember her age. Next year, she will finally stop driving (maybe). This year, her 1975 Dart sedan broke down on the freeway and rightaway, a few cars stop to *mālama* my mother and her senior sisters. The men fix the car and then it breaks down again on the surface streets. Aunty Alma calls Triple A and the big Portuguese tow truck guy comes and in squeeze the three ladies. Aunty Marjorie, the skinniest, is forced to sit next to the guy who is (of course) sweating, and Aunty Alma sits next. My mother sits next to the door because she needs to be free. She needs to be able to jump if need be. She is always worrying.
I told her, "Worry twenty-three hours a day, let one go." But Mildred, all her life expertise in worrying (**Never** on time, **always fifteen to thirty minutes before**

**schedule**), compromised her deficiencies by defending that "Playing poker is my only recreation"—as for her daughter, ideas are my "only recreation."

The "other" mother's house was much much more "civilized" and culturally developed. There was a piano, a library, a phonograph. Tai Yi, my mother's eldest sister in-charge, would now and then open up secret closets and peel out brocades, silks, silver dollars, jade. There was an altar in the kitchen and another outside on the spreading veranda under the lichee tree. There were so many *ono* violet and heavenly white, spidery yellows and green brown orchids. And mango trees and star fruit and a white peach tree and sugarcane and an avocado tree and a pomelo tree And a *pīkake* bush whose branches she would occasionally break off and shred the leaves. Breaking the wind with whip-like gestures, imagine how That was used (on my fat legs)! Everything, Everything was good. The food, always yummy. There were five cousins to babysit me—five different adventures per week. Was I "spoiled" early in life? Was that how life would be? Nelia was a daredevil, first to own a 35-mm camera and visit Europe! Egypt! the mainland!—where were these places? Honolulu was flat. Then there was Beatrice who played the piano. On days when I was being punished or just watching the air, Beatrice might start fooling around with Tchaikovsky and I would be instant mango slurp. I am still in love with Stanley who promised me the moon and became the archetype for every young man thereafter, and Jimmy his younger brother was "the baby." Florence was the corporate exec in the making, and I love my five cousins who crusaded my imagination, desires, and flooded me with over-expectation in this life.

## *Aloha!* Hello Ni *hao*

One afternoon, Tai Yi began to rap in our secret Hakka language for me to run and hide in the back bedroom. She drilled and bolted doors and windows. She sealed the drapes and lace curtains. "Get under the bed! Get in the back!" she commanded.
Not me, I needed to see. What was so urgent? "Get under the bed!?"—What kind of holocaust was happening? I never saw my cooking-and-washing-clothes aunt so crazy except when she was behind the wheel and somebody was cutting her off.
"You goddamn sonavabitch!" she'd cheerlead, "I have 'children' in this car, are you blind!?"

But we were in the house not the car. She was frantic when she saw how obstinate I was. "You brain-damaged squash! Heaven have mercy on this nitwit!"

This was no time for discourse. And then she pulled my collar to the floor while we peeked through the venetian blinds of the parlour. There was the mystery: it was a dark thing. What was it? "That," she explained, "was a black demon." What was a black "demon"? I saw a black "man"; he was black, but where was the "demon"? Following this incident, I continued to be dim about this matter and whenever I overheard someone refer to "niggah pits," I wondered about all the letters between A and Z. Mothballs later, I sensed that "niggah," "pits," and "black demon" belonged to a similar genre. However this was mere *idea*, not fact. There seemed to be a number of predicate adjectives and potential synonyms, but I was lost without a Subject. Such as "po po lo." *Popolo* was a dark sweet berry and/but *popolo* also had another meaning which was "black person." But no one explained this to me—like most complicated things, I had to visualize this out and, as they say in therapy, for myself. Moreover, since I had seen only one black person in my entire sheltered life while growing up in Hawai'i, this came slow. Slower than air.

## Traditions

My family hates change.

Everytime I was temporarily enchanted with some narcissistic function, some Voice would define me as "just like the father's side."

What did that *mean*?

Books later, while on my usual family huntdown, I discovered that it was a historical footnote meant to net me with my father's "scandalous" cousin Robert Wilcox who led a revolt against annexation in 1889. It meant that I had WHITE blood—or at least Hawaiian blood, Hawaiian party genes, and was capable of *poi* dog (leagueof nations) unpredictability.

It meant that I didn't know my place.

It meant whatever it was supposed to mean for the moment.

But I was no psycho/therapist, no CEO, no judge, not an adult, I was no match for the Voices.

What I could do was climb the *lichee* tree.

I talked to the branches.

The leaves with their heavy eyelids shook their heads and sighed.

And orchids shared their deepest secrets.

I hung upside down and listened to the sky.
When you twisted the arms of these *Hawaiian kine* bushes, antlers appeared instantly, so Bambi and I were longtime soul mates.
Then I lay on the veranda and listened to the soft wood singing me to sleep.

It was law that I "could not go beyond the boundary of the property," and an interview was required before anyone could play with me.
My world was the compound: the family and my uncontrollable mind.

## Two Lady Scholars

When I mentioned my family and no change, I especially mean being hypnotized one day by my mother and my Vogue-model Aunty (Scan Bones) Marjorie propitiously sipping tea up at the heights. There was all of Honolulu, the beach—a vistaview as locals say—to enjoy from the mountain homefront where the two watchdogs of culture were staring at the bay. Trying to locate the Pink Lady, there were "too many condos."
"Waikīkī is like Vegas."
"Uug, it's occupied by the Japanese."
"No, We're Not tourists. We have *nothing* to do with Waikīkī."
And then they began to blame Neil Armstrong for Everything. "Mildred," Aunty Marjorie confided, "everything on earth is ruined now." Completely sympathetic and willing to switch subjects, my mother leans over. "Too much change," she volunteers as a transitional phrase. "Since that Armstrong 'walked' on the moon, the Goddess is raped." This is the tricky part because here, my mother switches to their secret Hakka language, which is so underground that they use it only within the family to express profound insight and gossip. This Daedalus technique initiated me into and trained me for translation-code crackdown: foremost, allowing verbs "to be" and not be static for agreements with singular or plural government; b) stretching my ears while recalling all the gossip and philosophy sessions; c) considering the shortcomings of my mother and aunt; and d) factoring in their addiction to replaying the same tape altering one phoneme to revise the entire plot. With that in mind, I eavesdropped.
"The moon, the sun, and the stars were Never meant to be touched by man."
"Who do these people think they are? And then they come *here* to vacation."

"You watch, Pele's gonna geeve 'em hell!"

Aunty Marjorie, Miss Perfect, hath spoken, and mother, the younger (smarter) sister supports Aunty Marjorie. Which is Tradition in the finest sense of the word, not too smart, but repetitive and operational.

## Issues in Translation

Speaking for the Indians of the planet, we from Hawai'i grew up *lōlō* according to Robert's Rules and His Majesty's English. Our motto is "The life of the land is preserved in righteousness": *Ua Mau Ke Ea O Ka 'Āina I Ka Pono.*

Can you say that? We speak a little funny. Sometimes, we don't end sentences, but I met a German guy who did the same thing. Anyway, Hawai'i was different before statehood, and people from Hawai'i felt righteous just like the state motto about protecting what we got and where we came from. I mean, we're not so sure about English and everything else associated with it, but we're stubborn about being Hawaiian. Everybody that flew in after 1959 failed orientation. I'm just saying this because people go to My hometown and say, "I luv Hawai'i" like they are practicing English. The Hawai'i that they are luving is not *ono*, not good-eating buggah. That nouveau Hawai'i brought Shame to us Hawaiians. Everybody *says* they like oldtime Hawai'i, but it is tooourista supafares, condo-matic, best *pakalolo*, waterfront, property, hollywood dildos and bimbos that is the new artifice: Hawai'i. Hawaiians—and I means, the born and raised brownbloods—no like it when some *haole* comes to visit and writes something about Us! Cognitive Dissonance, braahh. Why doesn't somebody rebut? Why should we! Not Hawaiian style. As I was saying to my buddy Travis, I have an Indian mentality. When I was a kid and helplessly watched all those cowboys killing my guys, it was religious: white humans are stuck and threatened that maybe, they don't always know what's good for everybody. And I don't get why they need to "adopt" other cultures—become expert in all areas of ethnic culture.

That guy Vanilla Ice is a caricature of himself. In Oakland, white humans (Chinese too) are always entertaining themselves by pretending to be MC from Oaktown.

In Hawai'i, whites like to practice pidgin. They sound so stupid. They need to enroll in a Fundamental Pidgin class and get credit somehow. *haole* for you

## Why Folks from Hawai'i Have a Different Collective History from the Other States (of consciousness)

People have come a long way from the bow and arrow, but I can predict that some literary critic, some Chinese, somebody from my family will question—(not just "question" but complain and not just complain, but complain viciously)—question my intent in expressing these little questionable edges.

My mother will confusingly stare at me and wonder,

"Why, why did somebody so smart as you write such lousy English?

You spent $3000 on that computer and what?"

And, I still have that *Hawai'i Pono'i* mentality. You can tell by my *wala'au* yakkyyak style that I'm an American and I value my passport (especially in Zhong Guo), but to tell the truth, I don't know or feel anything about the "rockets red blare" or the "bombs bursting in air." I'm jess not inter-ested. And it's a war song; no kissing or hugging.

I know "King Kamehameha, the conqueror of the islands, became a famous hero one day." I know the "Hawaiian War Chant."

Sure these are military songs too but da beat man, and you can dance to these songs and feel sexual. Of coss, I know mo but lik Bu La'ia said, "iss one album."


My friend, Neaulani—the prettiest, smartest, nicest—nicest person was accepted into the *ahupua'a* when she was a very young woman. Not any conventional passage: (I was told by Lolly that) she faced herself at the same *pali* that Kamehameha pushed his enemies down one by one. Neau's mother Aunty Imgard wrote my father's favorite song, "*Pua Mana*." My sister danced with 'Iolani Luahine but then, the *hula* was underground because Hawai'i was in post-statehood shock.

We were ashamed.

because **THEY**— the *haole* and wannabe *haole* SAID You Hawaiian so

"stupid" "lazy": backward.

I bet you din't know we were ashamed, huh? because Hawai'i Visitors Bureau—can you beelieve they still keep the "Bureau" part in their name?

because the Bureau still putting our happy hour faces on

# EVERyTing that =

HAWAI'I.

Those dummies at the bureau so stoopid.

*Haole* complained day and night about "bad service."—All the cousins from my Chinese grandma's twelve kids have made the bucks: kids going to Punahou, Iolani, St. Andrews Priory—only private school—big houses, real estate—nobody speaks Chinese, knows eny-ting Chinese or desires any Chinese culture. They are ("practically," I've heard described) bizzy busy making money: buying things so they and progeny can live just like folks on the mainland. Next, dey goin have therapy and den maybe somebody going admit dey gay. Or sombody goin "convert"—heh, heh *convert* to *haole* kine buddhism. Meanwhile, all kine *haole* keep coming to Hawai'i, buy land, build big security gates to live imitation local lives. Kick da Ha-waiians off dey land. Hawaiians so happy, we no need nah-ting.

My husband described my living aunts and uncles as the Supreme Court. Another day, he referred to them as the dinosaurs. My aunties are exercising to keep the universe in shape. Mildred, the mathematician, does daily *wu shu* and drives her sedan just to keep alert. They all know that when they die, Nobody will go to the temple. Nobody will know how to order at the restaurants. Nobody will speak our funky secret language again. We will be out of stories because we assimilated. And my Hawaiian cousins—*'auē*, we have trashed and cleaned the desktop on that folder long ago. Booo. but we comin back brah *Kānaka* comin back—lucky for everyOne else

**All these aspects were present (though not discussed) during the Friday night poker game which began as a diversion during the war.**

## Island Physics

Although I know that one plus one matter of factly equals two ones, conscientiously, I could not apply that "reasoning" to this document: those of us from Hawai'i and anyone else who grew up "mainland-ized," "*haole*-fied"—"marginalized" is what it's now called—we were supposed to be textbook right and ethnically "traditional." This process cannot happen without a lot of *lōlō* (Hawaiian for dummY) flying loose. When I read and enter James Joyce's reality or Virginia Woolf's politics or Willa Cather's daily accounts of ordinary folks or William Blake's celebration of the grain of sand, I talk myself into exposing a pervasive being intimidated, challenged, and flourishing in the chaos of my formal and informal education while growing up in a "territory."

Words like "territory" or "reservation," "rancheria"—lose historical meaning if some insecure loudmouth like myself doesn't write down why people who grow up under these unique systems are truly *sui generis*. Which is not better: I do know how to eat with knives and forks. And I eat with chopsticks, my hands. I also eat with my feet! If you are uneasy with this concept, maybe you are imagining that I am hoping you will feel guilty by my saying things. What you really need to do is to see all the Cassavetes movies. One by one, flick after flick in the dark—and Gena Rowlands is Ahmazzing to look at—you will see, sometimes, genius looks like crazy or idiocy.

**And now there's Yolanda: she remembered 1A. 2B. She remembered and can see. You will hear more about her.**

NOTES: for those who require a translation: read Heidegger's Nietzsche, "The Law of Contradiction That Commands."

## *ONO ONO* GIRL'S MODULAR PHILOSOPHIES

In the midst of passion, humans become poetic, *sometimes*. There is a difference between a lawyer and a poet. When I was linked to my Old Friend, I guess he loved me, but he always had to be Right. It got so that I was always looking words up in the dictionary just for standard meaning. That wanting-to-be-middle-class mediocre *haole* had to be right. But when people get desperate, they don't need to be right, they just need to feel like they belong to some general order of things. You see this all the time in the courts. People begin to disguise language and alter common meaning to redistribute the wealth of ambiguity. This is the reason that I became interested in Nominalism. Anyway, when people become desperate, they begin to use language like poetry. Nouns become perfect verbs. Dangling preps without objects are unnoticed and new concepts are invented. It is quiet and revolutionary but standard linguistic policy. The books on grammar and composition were my early passions. I loved Spelling in elementary school. I loved diagramming sentences. I had affairs with Latin.

The world is shrinking and still Some people are relying on Spellcheck to counteract racism. See what I mean? We are using the wrong "utilities" to express this imbalance, our disappointments, our rage. I love the concept of God, but God is not the answer: we need to love disorder and appreciate the fundamental dissonances it provides in the context of vision.

Singing loud and maybe even off key needs to be loved—not merely accepted as a given: let those folks who want to sing but too shy to—Go ahead and express your own enthusiastic art form! C'mon, they know they are not the **soloist**—a word that the *haole* brought with their hymns and god—*ONO ONO GIRL* says, "Sing! Sing"

## Secrets

Now, I'll "share" my life with alcoholism. I don't know if I'm an alcoholic. I don't drink all the time meaning: everyday—before I get into my car or on the job. I drink when I'm scared. I drink when I'm angry. At least, I used to drink when I felt hurt. Anyway, I thought I'd write about my wine and T & T love affair because Asian Merican lit is not writing about the William Burroughs aspect of drilling deep into daily life.
—It was reassuring and insightful to watch all the women drinking in The Summer House (love that Jeanne Moreau) and I love to watch Gena Rowlands drink on the screen.
Women who drink are trying to locate themselves.
Our breasts are so beautiful.
Our necks so tender and wanting to love and be loved.
*Regarde* our wrists! so willing to carry and serve
And there is nothing finer than a woman's back which she is willing to bend or break as she pursues the common canon of her male-designed image

The language of men simply does not fit the bodies of women—try to substitute a garbage disposal for the acoustic microscope and see what kind of "performance" results.

I never drank until I met an old friend: his family is Tall and they all drink everyday anytime (not a cliché). He always introduced his family as the Tall is Superior type and *lōlō* me anticipated some real "conversation," "interaction," "sensitivity group." What I got was a bunch of uptight, racist, Christian drunks. They lived in "Blaund"—what a name! and the people all behaved like Blaunders.
I "hadto" bond with the Blaund mother by drinking gin and tonics early in the morning (while she made ice cubes then pressured me into K-Mart entry-level prattle) until I began to hate my own self.

Hey! everything is developmental, right? I still didn't learn.

After the Old friend, there was Ross, the sensitive, big-brown-eyed musician boyfriend who smoked dope all the time, so then, I picked up the intoxicating *marijuana*. The Drinking: everybody who is or hangs out with musicians knows the link between alcohol, drugs—sex and music. Happy musicians make happy music. Booze, drugs, sex, the eternal opiates. They're all so good together. Anybody who says no is a liar. I'm not a fan of anything beyond marijuana but a good attractive body and "extra help" equals cheap fun.

Looking back, it's kind of interesting to see that I started drinking for Dick and Dick's mother so they could laugh all through the day. And then (to be a good girl) later I smoked dope to keep my musician boyfriend company while making Him feel normal! Drinking was so "normal" among these good Americans. My own family drank only at nine-course Chinese dinners. Johnny Walker Black Label standard. I ought to buy a bottle of that shit just for sentimental reasons. Poor me, talk about accommodation! Talk about dedication!

What can stop the mechanisms of life from being, right? I need to be living it. At my "evolved" stage, my China husband doesn't like any drinking or drugs, but how he loves to break dishes and smoke cigarettes:
can you begin to guess what I'm now up to?

## HOw *ONO ONO* GIRL Began to Fail as Chinee Wife

The whole idea for my mouth to open up to my head was to probe the subject of gambling.

—You know that recent execution-murder of that loan shark's wife and daughter? Rumora seem to spell out the guys who did it. How about that murder in Chinatown a couple of months ago? The gossip was good, but who knows? And you know what else? The artist Bob told my friend Nancy how while he was lunching with a certain mayor of a certain artsy city, the mayor says how the State Attorney General's office is gonna investigate these guys that my Great Love yaks with in Chinese. After one of our celebrated fights, as he is pounding down the door, I leak this in formation to him and (of course) he doesn't bother with what inside information Artists might be privy to. But funny how the miracle of art spins: a few days later my Great Love is busily translating and creating answers for these scar-faced, soft-skinned criminals.

Limp, guys, morons, the military—I hate them—will always exist: what pisses is that my guy, the baby, is the runner; lackey to these punchless creeps. At best, they drive (very badly) a Mercedes and flash gold. These are the lowliest, the typical Chinaswines: their spit airborne as the volume of noise enhances their aura. *Nouveau riche* peasants digging the nose with cash. These are the reasons why China girls are marrying white so quick. Sure, Asians marry white for upward mobility—what? this is news? Chinese boys, Chinese mothers: there is an outdated myth that Chinese boys are Chinese emperors. But, some people still practice stupid ideas because there Must be dummies on earth. The PG&E Energy Saving guy called it, "balancing out." Gamblers are the idiot savants of rectal management. No one pays attention to statistics: the house always wins. Losing money and dreaming of winning is actually some kind of fun (forgive me, my entire family, especially my mother). On the other hand, most people would condemn Me for "gambling" on writing as a career because it is certainly an occupational hazard in and of itself. But at least I leave a legacy for my kids to cry or laugh over—or maybe believe that Carolyn had developed hood ornamentcy into an art.

My husband, my Great Love always refers to me as a legend when he is not accusing me of biting him (I was born in the Year of the Dog). My father's biggest gamble was that I would be a boy and, lucky for him, I saved him from gambling any further. My husband used to gamble and lost our 'ōkole. We had some fights.

The police have come to the house a number of times.
Now he "says" he doesn't gamble—probably still does and we still do fight.
When I reach page 158 I will "share" the tragedy of John Good with you. He is the main reason why I began to write this but I need to protect you from falling too deep into the ocean too soon. John Good is the true contemporary immigrant story that you don't read or hear about. He is the saddest sack: a compulsive/obsessive liar. A lazy parasite, so painful to write about it because in doing so, I need to justify his life in some way. To know about John Good means you are aware that—Chinese in America—is the laundered version of Chinese. Maybe you will feel that it is a lie.
But,
I will write about John Good so you can see into my own life as the wife of an immigrant—
definitely a life
but not without insult,

tears,
and much
much despair.

## *ONO ONO* GIRL and the PERFECT China-in/outlaws

My in-laws showed up today. Bilingual-pilingual: it's a game. I have been to China three times, hell and heaven every time. And I sweated through Madarin while acquiring carpal tunnel syndrome. Properly, I prepared: by being criticized while reading all the "right" classical down to the communist books and magazines. I went to lectures, was insulted, and saw movies. Stared at (because I didn't know squat-toilet etiquette and took off my pants Before squatting over the well of dung and waste). I was hissed at while fingers pointed to me. I ate the funky food with the flies hovering about. When Mildred warned that I was proving to be an idiot again, I had a mild inclination I was entering danger.

Husband-side mother-in-laws have special status. "His" mother, supposedly a college-educated teacher—why didn't She anticipate and understand the need to speak Yinglish before arriving in America? Mom and pop are in deep trouble during the first moments in my house and I like foreigners! But just who do these people believe they are as they peel green onions on the floor of my living room! They arrived fumed in mothballs with large kitchen knives and blankets. Why didn't their prince my husband prepare them? **I hate these people**: they make me feel like Arthur Waley who after sailing to and arriving at China refused to get off the boat because he didn't want his dream/China to be destroyed. I know I sound like a redneck, but in the state of the arts time of electronic toys; in light of the Chinese capacity of mind over matter; these in-laws being here is an act of anarchy: there are no clues or rules. Heraclitus-intense, there is no order.

The best part is that my mother diligently lectures via telephone on "being nice to his parents." When Mildred, the modern-day feminist confucianist, arrives for Thanksgiving dinner, she will blow a fuse. Having done China before I was born and once or twice post Uncle Mao, each time before I left for Zhong Guo, she warned me that it was a dump.
Now, all of a sudden, reality is sobering me up and Mildred, entitled as ever, remains my personal hood ornament, seeing the Void topsy turvey; practicing

*wu shu;* loving her half-white (translated: "shit") granddaughters; giving notice to anyone in her path.

I do not know how to be thoroughbred girl-docile serving everyone Chinese. I have imagined that I am and have been Chinese for at least a steady ten to fifteen years; but all it takes is a brand new load of "immies" to show up, and either the world has not progressed since the 1900s, or these invaders have some kind chutzpah.
Is it too much to ask that my mother-in-law not paw me to show affection?
And, is it unjust that I request my father-in-law not speak to me like I *am* Chinese?
Hey? why don't I just start rapping *en francais* and see if he gets my drift?
If a sentimental sinophile condemns me by explaining that this is not a "Chinese thing," that it is an old folks thing, then these folks should die young like they used to.
Take a look at the Russians: do you think the ballet and Dostoyevsky would adjust their economy? Piaget is the one they should be listening to. Step by step, buddy.

My husband says that Americans are too liberal: that if a cop asks, "What did the burglar look like?"
You, who have been victimized, see "yellow, white black or orange" but report, "tall, fat; wore a green hat."
Therefore, I tried to use my husband's own criteria to illustrate similarity in the Chinese way of being illusive deeply imbedded in the system of saving face. I tried to address this at length but he denied everything.
American, artist, or merely just Carolyn Lau, I seem to be the direct sort. I hate wasting time and I want results. This business of lying to save face is inefficient. Why waste time lying? It's endemic to Chinese (Irish too): they don't even know that they're lying they're such conditioned sociopaths. On top of this, they are Expecting to find gold mountain!
Isn't this a bit dated?—Don't they have a kind of *Time* or *People* magazine back there?

Nobody calls San Francisco Gold Mountain anymore (get it? "GM" as in what Chevrolet *used to* mean) except maybe a paragraph at most in a kid's history book.
Here I am
approaching the Principle of Uncertainty from the angle of Nominalism and

I am expected to teach immigrant sixty-year-old kindergartners after three o'clock for free!

I am a woman, insecure about a lot of stuff but a slave, no.

Sometimes, I wonder about those missionaries in Hawai'i—did they in fact teach some practical skills in terms of contracts and time management?

I know that I am not a redneck. I know that I am not a racist—unknowingly I was when I was a kid and early on as an adult, but what I profited from my in-laws being here is that I value my space.

I value my limited resources.

I would never go into someone's home and operate Merely according to my instincts.

The standard here is America in the electronic age. Anyone can come here, but why should the immigrant drain our resources without actively contributing? And, I am *beginning to feel* that everyone here should speak English. If I were to go to Beijing and only hide out with the Americans, that would be considered elitist—should we therefore call the newcomers elitists? separatists? isolationists?

Immigrants—Latinos, Ethiopians, French—cannot hide under that term if they want to survive in my hood.

You can only imagine what I have to say on the matter as a *kanaka*!

## Vision 2: The Intertextual Confession of an Algebra/Latin Addict

> My first libido-driven piece of writing as a child was based on Tampax magazine ads; my second piece was a play with girls and boys dressing up as nuns and priests imitating the Mass.

> Question: are these examples of inductive or deductive (aka reductive) reasoning?

A. I'm pretty sure that the truth is that (until my mother told me that she loved me this past Christmas Eve) *I've forced myself to operate like a boy.*—Maybe that's why I like *mahu* (homosexual) so much: I've never felt like a boy but ye olde private school trained me to COMPETE, Answer Back; "Don't get mad, get even"; **SABOTAGE feelings** and focus like a mature man (yeah yeah).

I wrote those pain-in-the-heart Chinese poems anxiously waiting for Ariadne to slit my footnotes in the shape of a Chinese sheep.

Chinese: language, philosophy, culture, gods, with women crawling-in-last-pecking after mother-in-laws; Chinese is a guy-thing. Except for Hakka because we are the enigmas, the mutants, the On-Our-Owns. As a Hakka Hawaiian, I have no idea what "obedience" means and do not care if I do not know how to spell it either.

All those "ence" "ion" words freak me because it's like holding air. What are the actions of these sounds?
I suppose they mean about the same as "First Son" in Chinese.
First Son may as well mean "only son" which according to the medical dictionary is defined as

No perspective, Spo-oiled Brat, parasite, psychopath, party poop.

Being a girl—a "curious" "thinking" "overly sensitive" "bad girl" at that—no one gave me a clue as to consequences of what "First" combined with "Son" resonates, provides, entitles and enslaves a penis. After my Great Love and I were fighting and I complained to my mother that he was so this and so that, she said,
"Well, isn't he the First Son?"
"What does that mean?" I delicately questioned.
"He's the First Son," emphasized my mother through the wires of the telephone.
"Welll, what does the 'First Son' mean?"
"You know Chinese," she despaired without the words to explain.
Do I???? I had been self-imprisoned studying, studying Chinese; trying, enslaving myself to be Chinese, but did I lack the basic knowledge of
"The being-ness of Chinese"? What a big question? Was there something—or worst—
Nothing to "being Chinese?"
And me! I was trying to communicate with a Chinese, a Chinese male, a Chinese First Son. I had an epidemic in my body. Only now, my mother thought to have this "heart to heart" chat with me? Was she such a great mathematician that I appeared like a number in her life so that only now, it occurred to her that I didn't know some "stuff" that was natural to her—heh heh, but foreign to Me?

I can think and act like a guy because my parents ordered me that way. I do poems the way my mother does taxes. Outside the job, I favor my father— not wasting time with self-promoting talkers. Daddy commonly, commonly advised,

"Not my *kuleana*." Not one breath or synapse of his concern.

Ask my family or one or two friends: I can get along with guys a lot better now because I know how to think male better than any dry penis. Talk general sports, talk cars; reference one or two simple items: you don't have to work very hard with a guy.

Women have "feelings" which they can rarely express and when they do it is usually bad because we are called "hysterical" or "crazy" when we do. No mo practice, no good, eh. So traditionally, women cook and coo and shove the knife in the guy's butt while he's taking the shit; that is, the woman artfully produces a hemorrhoid or ulcer in a male when she cannot order her emotions "subject, verb, object" like saying "coffee, toast, butter on the side." Being a woman, she might even say "please," and if she wasn't brutalized too much that day, she'll even smile.

A couple of years ago, I was mumbling to myself (silently, of course) like a baglady: G-uys are always insulting me as the ultimate challenge—that's only because a guy cannot even remember to turn off a light after he has flipped the switch. Can he remember to close a gate? or pick up the orange peels on the floor which he delivered as he watched television?

What do guys know about the subjunctive????? and the ones who do, don't have a clue about fucking. Keep them in the fields. Throw them some beer now and then. Let them be privy to all the James Bond movies. The He-men will be content.

Latino is a guy thing too: Rickey is like my transcendental corridor. He let me be me without penalty. The penultimate matador castanetting, cavorting, whining; slicking his hair, palms, and cheeks with coconut oils; Rickey is lighting altars with gardenias to owls amidst *duende*. His jade peak, second to a calcifiedwalrus throttle, is the size of Alaska oozing Texacana petro poems.

I threatened him with the idea that maybe he could write poems, but could he write a sentence?

This insult interrupted his one-foot de-planing while he prepared to blitzkrieg the next crowd in yet another state, another poetry reading, *un autre* Rickey poetry colony. Anyway, Rickey taught me the art of Porto Rican doodoo as well as learning to forgive and making the most of acting dumb. A twinkling critical thinker—a little fat like a lot of us now—but, as we say in Hawai'i, "class."

Rickey can only be buddies with me. The last time I saw him he shouted "You analyze the puff outa shit." The other memorable quote is "Do you think I parked the car okay?" I thought it was fine. "You know, I don't know with you. If you ws a meter maid, you might consider giving a ticket because I didn't park the car according to 'The Rules.' "

With the exception of m' gay brahs, I'm limited. "As a woman" I find it difficult to imagine being "intimate" with "guys" because they don't have periods and are privileged to create illusions about life. They don't raise the kids. Maybe Now, it's trendy for the YUPPY daddies to push strollers and change disposable diapers, but long-term? During WWI, women were asked to work in factories, wear pants, grease machines. In the Women's Movement, women are *encouraged* to pull and drill teeth; bust balls in court; deliver the sermon in church; engineer designs.

When in history has there been a national or international call for men to process like women? Not merely exchange jobs for a day, I mean wholly experience the processes and joys of womanhood? With the exception of the neighborhood local god Apollo Cyril Gulassa, Edsel Matthews, Mr. Koncepts, and my gay friends, the secret is that men are either unequipped or overprotected: scared to give birth to what a guy should have evolved to by now and Robert Bly is clueless to what that means. Viva menstruation! *Hola* Empress Menopause!

## Mona Lisa Grandma

Every writer has a couple of Grandma or Gramps vignettes. I am no exception. My *tūtū*, my Hawaiian-Portuguese grandma danced the *hula*, mostly was soft-spoken and graceful like all Hawaiian *kūpuna* I know. Regrettably I wasn't born in time to be carried and sung to in Hawaiian—because she only spoke Hawaiian—and feel like I missed a major blessing in my life. My "other" grandma was certainly a bedfull of screams. She wore an invisible visor. She was a majordomo.

When she lived in that big dark house on School Street, she'd sweep the cool wood floor yakking in those underground tones.

Often, my Tai Yi would join in the yak yuk dok nga zing bang dong while I enviously dreamed to someday be included as a trio.

One day, PoPo was visited by her friend/relative/in-law/husband's side, Ah Hoi Moi as called by Grandma. Ah Hoi Moi had these intense mango breasts beneath her upper-class Chinese dress. I kind of enjoyed sneaking looks of her firecracker eyes and hearing her emphasize particular concepts with grandma. But grandma didn't want me around, knowing she couldn't trust me in public. *I might just influence her.*

With nothing to do except chase monkeys in the mango trees, tea with ladybugs in the garden, or watch the sun dry the overwashed clothes on the line, I sniffed parsley.

I began understanding mynah birds.

Eventually, I wanted to be with grandma. You know the type, tie myself around her arm or leg. Not so much that after twelve kids and a tough life she was amazingly beautiful but she smelled good and I liked the way she dragged me. It was her combination of ripe mangoes and jasmine flowers powered into a thin bone frame.

She never kissed me or hugged me but I am Granma's favorite.

For years, I was tormented that my own mother did not love me because she, too, did not hug or kiss me. But back on that day when Ah Hoi Moi was loudly blaring through her big buck teeth, there was a fly.

"Ah Hoi Moi, Ah Moi Hoi, da wu yin!"
without warning, I alarmed.
"Hoi girl, Hoi girl, kill the fly."

The missing part is that while it is acceptable for people Hoi girl's age (about fifty then) to call her that, little fat babies—especially the ones that attend "private school"—should have been educated otherwise. Days later, my mother (after clucking in horror with her sisters) confronted me with this *faux pas* that reflected a failure on my mother's part to educate me in "the ways." The irony was that until I began coercing my mother to practice Hakka with me, she never even spoke Chinese to me. It was up to the five-star Tai Yi to have provided *that* incidental because Tai Yi lectured me in Hakka from the moment I entered her house.

Nonetheless, Mildred began her task.

To make her lecture short, I was supposed to call Aunty Mango Breasts "Ah Ho Sau" to show respect. But I was a kid and used to hearing the name Ah Hoi Moi whenever gossip or Ah Hoi Moi showed up. Fearing the varied and potential combinations of inexcusable excitement, thereafter, I never attempted her name. If I saw her, I hid. When I was older, I smiled and now Ah Ho Sau is with grandma—I guess.

More on grandma. After an accident which left her paralyzed in both legs, she may have slowed down, but not the laughs.
Every Sunday afternoon, my mother and I would drive to grandma's new big digs on the hill.
Those were some of the times when Aunty Marjorie and Mildred would philosophize.
In her bedroom, I would pull grandma's wispy bun while teasing her about turning bald!
Routinely, I would challenge her to Chinese checkers.
While neither of us knew how to play *this* game
it was understood that checkers was perfunctory to the payoff of me always winning.
While we never wagered any bets, the winner was to pay me in silver dollars. Heavy fifty-cent pieces and thick silver dollars rolled out of grandma's cardboard box.
Never enough! Grandma was too cheap!
I was worth more!
How does a hostage of pleasure respond but to give in?!
Grandma always had to have the full treatment. She was no wimp. She'd allege that I was a crook. She accused me of cheating.
Was I to allow her these disgraceful charges!
First, I would crank the hospital bed on the backrest side, then I would equalize the feet so that grandma would be in a V position hollering, shouting, cursing.

Where were the daughters as this "abuse" continued?
The daughters drank tea. One filed her nails while the other twitched. Sometimes, they would cut gardenias or orchids or blue ginger or pick avocados or mangoes. They would look at the ocean from their mountain retreat and in between sighs, complain. They never came to grandma's rescue. They knew grandma (didn't want to be bothered).

## More and Less Chinese

I presume that it's inevitable I will *again* address the thorn in my face, the Chinese. As I told my husband—when I had one—the book on China is CLOSED.

Maybe it was and has been my bad luck, but the Chinese are mean (or maybe just inexperienced) and don't know how to be warm. I know I'll get pelted for that but just take a walk in any Chinatown anywhere and check out the scowls on their faces.

Why is their forehead ALWAYS in an eternal wedge?

Are they scared? Are they nervous?

Why do they look so contracted?

Why do they stare? and for a people who are supposed to be so smart, they don't Even know they staring!

(you know) Why I not interested to return to where there is no *there* and study another morpheme about the place or people?

Good ting I found out I ws Hawaiian in time. And I couldn't even do in Hawai'i because I look so *pake* and my Chinese *'ohana* no like believe I could

Really BE Hawaiian—coss who wanted to be Hawaiian anyway? So I wass fossed to act upper clss Chineeese nice and could nevah be no Hawaiian. My darling friend, da famous and nicest nice, beautiful gracious warm humble good fun and *nui akamai 'ōlelo ā kahiko ā 'auana kumu* Naomi Kalama, said

"Good ting you came Kaleponi so you could finally be Hawaiian!"

# Forty-nine, not yet menopausal, and finally safe to be Hawaiian

Thank you *akua*, I no need to be Chinese all the time anymoa. NOT easy to be Chinese and no mo fuN can get.

And as far as the Middle Kingdom is concerned, I neveeer want to hear that calling up of the well (hooaahhtT) and see airborne wads, globs, fleeting clicks of spit projecting on or off target. I neeeever want to see that me?-huh?-it-just-feels-soo-goooD-to-be-digging-my-nose-that-I-do-it-anywhere-anytime. It's bad enough to be among the elite here who are more than my lifetime of stress management.

You want the truth? Here it is, which to the political correctionists will *sound* or *read* racist, but anyone who works within the nit and gritty of Chinese-beat-wife-and-kids, gamble, smoke smoke smoke, on the street, in your face immigrant *knows.* Chinese are among the most insecure jewels on the planet. The adults always competitive and complaining. I don't know if it's because, historically, the culture promotes cut-throat competition and that there is a pecking order with the freeze-dried wiener at the top. Men shout to women like men—or furniture at best. During Liberation, women went to bed as farm animals and as the ink was drying on the Sex Equalization Act the next AM, women metamorphosed into men. Women are an existential concept. Unlike Eurydice who had the good fortune of dumping Orpheus at marriage and cutting quite a cozy escape from the bondage of his lousy frogshit lines, Chinese women have to be good actresses at faking orgasm or at least good at panting and screaming exactly (or she will have to practice again and again until it is) the way her guy has seen it on Chinese television. Upon the arrival of Big Foot into *chez ton; toute de suite,* the just-married Mrs. Chinese Wife recycles criticism, ridicule, and insult into a smile. When she's older, she lays a fart. But while she's still accepting the art of suffering in silence, a good old Chinese girl must believe bitterness is the way of life. She's a magician with that, making lemonade from a lemondick parable, and unlike human beings who imagine heaven as a respite from earthly chaos, the Chinese make fiction out of life—Karl Marx.

Acting out empty spiritual lives; shoving gold crooked teeth and hazardous driving skills as contemporary Ah-Q's double-park thick BMW's and Mercedes to prove the worth of their accumulated bucks; things and more things gained atta bargain is Chinese.

Because they got their screws on wrong: China is countryside. Eight hundred million peasants multiplying fast-track. Still, everyone wants to go to the city. Remember footbinding? A fad that ruined women. Except for the Hakka women, they all bought into the idea that squashed, stinky broken bones equal beauty! It's like the land thing. All Chinese I know say how much they enjoy visiting the countryside even though life was tough. If a kid from the countryside makes it to Bei Da or even less than Beijing University, people always remark that he is *from the countryside* like it is Evil Itself.

(Tee hee) The Chinese believe they originate above earth, below heaven. Now, that lacks a sense of humor! It's tough to live up to that kind of ego planting. That's why they require so so much material crap. Walking barefoot and feeling the warm earth is a turn-on to a normal human but low-class to a Chinese. Too bad! *Tian ah!* Middle-Kingdomers are Madonna groupies—slaves of the material world: when they die it is a fact they return for more goodies as rats, cocks, snakes, swine, sheep, monkeys. The rabbits and dogs may evolve into birds. If you evolve into birds, you can then transform into fire, water, or air. From there, Chinese go to hell or face deportation to the Middle Kingdom.

The Chinese Americans—who used to not like the idea of a Chinese American restaurant not too many years ago—they will have plenty to gossip about my opinions. I will continue to be excluded from this or that Asian American event. But hardcore *Zhong Guo ren*, the Chinese, will be too busy shouting while counting money; playing mah jong and spitting out melon seeds; shuffling their footsies in Chinatown, their full faces frowning in deep concentration—they will not care or notice their profiles.

Last but not least are the altogether different breed, the Chinese Christians, who were Chinese in their last lives and are not the "99.9999% pure Han" hardcore animals. When they die, they get to take cars and houses, jade, manuals, and a little pork with them. The Chinese Christians they get to smile, singing, "This Land Is Your Land, This Land Is My Land," on or off key.

Is this person (New Age)/bitch (sexist) writer frustrated?—my musician boy-friend's favorite term for anyone who seemed on edge. I don't know if I'm so much frustrated as weary of all the Chinese American "then" vs. "now" rag being printed. There is a real "out West" flavor in the Chinese American psyche and that, therefore, would *seem* to manifest in the literature, but what I'm seeing more resembles yet another multicultural aka chop suey "exercise" I recently walked through.

We had to bond, name the place and origin of, name parents of, And give a name to a lemon (*and* associate that we were dealing with racism). We then had to accept or not accept a banana, coconut, or soft-inside apple. Everybody went along with this exercise because no one had the guts to say, "This is a waste of time," although there were those in the room just anticipating that I would blow everyone's kosher cover. Later, my Chinese friend from LA would say that for the Chinese 'mericans in the room, this was as far as they could muscle in terms of public confrontation. Be-(yawn)nign as it was, the whites and blacks were the spokeslemons. The Chinese saved face and graciously allowed the nails to be drilled into their creativity happily ever after. Eternally in that poetic Void, for the Chinese, when human feelings matter, the stages of contact are too remote.

Don't the Chinese have secret doors inside their psyches that they yearn to slide down into a pitcher of white light? Please! Besides Lu Xun, is there no one *other* among the billions—one Chinese that is wondering just *why things aren't so.* Ambitiously in essence, singular, they are collective. Perhaps that is their luck. Chinese are homogeneous. Maybe that's my problem. I want to be Chinese, but I never was nor can I ever be. Meanwhile, I *look* Chinese. For years, I have been claiming that my friend Reneé is my twin. We always get a kick because she is a big woman, very Nancy Wilsonish. I, on the other hand, am short, impatient, and blue. We have matching fuchsia-and-teal water pistols and look exactly alike, especially the glasses. After Labor Day this year, we also have artful Japanese wooden ear-wax cleaners—hers is nicer than mine.

## The Gospel According to Lani Moo

The miracles in my life have been the following:

1. Owl in my backyard
2. Mother as a hood ornament
3. The Gorilla/Bird
4. Meeting Guan Yin and my affair in China
5. *Kanaka*

Other highlights:

1. C-sections, my girls, And
   Watching them shape themselves into women
2. Getting a divorce from their father
3. On and off Chinese
4. Loving my husband and living without him
5. (Trying to) killing myself

*In the nineties, god does not reveal God(s) like the Bible or in the way it is still taught by ordained men. The books and men have described akua all wrong.*

When I was a fetching young woman, all I wanted was a full auditorium of screaming fans catcalling and mad for my poetry. Christ! I was in the ballet studio every day. For fun, I studied Chinese and brushpainted. That kind of dream suppression was an extension of my high school days when I wanted nothing short of letting the boys see my panties as a cheerleader; but I was too busy being the Moon Goddess associating
**only with Chinese**
and acting one's age was looked down upon.
We postured.

We had our names and faces in the society section of the newspaper every weekend—weekdays sometimes.

I was known for my extraordinary eyebrows. Out of boredom, I began hanging out with the surfers. Began to drink (expensive whiskey, what else: beer was for low class).

Within a month, I was sick of shopping. The boys were cute, drove their daddies' very fancy cars: we all had that phony prep school voice where your inner throat is poised for sarcasm or rejection. Our collective unconscious equaled a fencepost or maybe a dead chicken. We had our family names to protect. Reputation. So, I curled into a down-sweep of rejection and failure when I began to ask for More from my Chinese boyfriend. Eventually, the gang advised Reynold to drop me.

The armies followed: Singapore gang member Paul who drove the biggest fuckin car in the world. I should have known that I was in trouble that summer when all those college boys were smelling tail but I was so damn into my image that I had no sense of my Pau-wa. Beverly told me I could have Ehny guy—and come to think of it—I did. All the cute and/or rich Chinese guys dated me: they dropped from the sky. I changed outfits and went to nightclubs. I made out in (their) daddy's Lincoln Continental.

There was the prim cute-looking dud at Columbia in Nuclear Physics, Francis "Franny" (can you believe that!) Fook, who took me out to a movie and I then proceeded to drink him "under the table." Francis never asked me out again. We never even got to the kissing stage. What was so cute about him?

When I look at the photos in my high school yearbook, I cannot believe how cute I was!

When I look at myself in the mirror now, I pretend that if I could only have another chance, I would die to be the Costco shopping wife of any of those Chinese guys with life insurance policies backed by CASH to count in the bank.

Who am I kidding? I would evaluate their limitations in one or two sounds!

But while it lasted, every year the San Francisco boys would come to Honolulu—Kenny Ching, Soupy, DJ, and even Gee Lau.

Later, I was in love with Daniel Chang. He grew up with me—the Iolani/Yale type and appreciative of me but you know me—I always wanted MMMOore. On my wedding day, my mother said

"Your father is so disappointed you didn't marry Daniel Chang." Too bad, she didn't let me know they liked him so much when I was dating him.

There were white boys in between—armies of white bread, then back to the China *mantou*, the hard no-tasting roll. For what? to find the embodiment of heaven on earth—man.
Failure after failure: no god in no man.
Did I listen accurately?
Did I misread the text?
Or, was there a misprint or misrepresentation of the oracle?
I waited, I served man. I prayed. I got lucky.
In my studies on Chinese philosophy, I came across a fatso named Zhuangzi who wondered if he was a butterfly or if the butterfly was Zhuangzi. Eureka!

*Is woman and the process of bonding and nurturing the source of spirituality and, therefore, eternity-immediate    or*

are man and his unproductive long-term solutions still the same old answer?

The biggest disappointment in self-discovery is learning that you have cleaned only the easiest and most simple congestion on the desktop lifetimes later when you are vis-a-vis, tete-a-tete to the leftovers from childhood: the Big Hurts, is there life after death? (hope not)

Yes. It follows forgiving the Big Ones, revisiting the moment of birth at death, and accepting that, ultimately, I was and will be alone. My body is a star. I will burn until I disappear. I will not return to the earth—some creatures need to, want to. I already have my feelings. There are no requirements, eligibilities, or references for eternity. All the fears and words that guys have written have been wrong. Heaven is a girl thing—"Not!" (Madonna)

## Prayer to Be Wished While Considering Suicide

Sweet Self
of what I see and how I hear
(outside the dance Thioridazine)

Will Blake, draw the ladder to the moon!
Cousin who promised owl in my body!
Sister who runs in me!

Sweet Daughters, Enitharmon's kiss protect you!
Dancing sister!
Daddy, o daddy

Sweet Gorilla/Bird, in bramble and petals my eyes
linger.

Little island my birth, Hawai'i
*kōkua.*
*Aloha nō.*

(so you think this is a bad poem. of course it is. I was fighting mySelf from killing me. of course, it sounds stupid. if you're gonna kill yourself, you don't run Spelecheck)

## Craig the Early Beat Influence

Gee, just when I was beginning to feel **mid-life crisis**, who calls but my childhood friend! A sweetie. He has CFO after his name on the letterhead stationery. I asked, "Just what do you do?" He says, "I'm the Treasurer (of Pigybank)." I know about as much of what that means as he does about a "career" as a poet. My husband is more impressed that my friend called me after not hearing my voice for thirty years! Twilight zone. Imagine *his imagination* when I sent him my book last year! At sixteen Craig had a crush on me: I was Karyle. Curled eyelashes, ladled-on mascara, fresh from braces teeth, shy on the outside, perfectly coifed from the tips of my hair to the matching shoes per outfit. If you look at my photos during this time, I really look pretty. Karyle in the social section of the newspaper "at another reception" on the weekends, during the week. Karyle Lau inventing her persona while maintaining the canon of her Hakka culture. Karyle Lau was the person I evolved into after not being able to *look* Hawaiian, *look* the English I supposedly was not, be close enough to be valued as Chinese. Carolyn simply adjusted the spelling of "Carol" to "Karyle" when I was about fourteen and *became* it until I was about nineteen when the poet Stan Rice insisted on calling me "Carolyn Lau." A couple of aunts insisted on calling me "Caroline"—some people that I meet now also hear "Caroline" and I let them call me that. Usually, they are foreigners. My Spanish friends almost all call me "Carolina." My darling, Mr. Powerhouse, Mr. Ichiban, my performer, my husband who calls me "Carolyn Lau" as though he were giving a dog a bone, has given up hope that I will convert to "Carolyn Xu." Meanwhile, he has changed his spelling from "X-u" to "S-h-u," which is easier when you're guessing to pronounce the $x + u$ combination. Most people say "Zoo" because probably they are thinking about "xerox." My students all call me "Miss Lau" because my mother is "Mrs. Lau." I will always be Carolyn Lau because it's been a mule's climb for me to realize how adorable, nasty, talented, and insecure I am. Viva! Right on! Shakka! Maybe, Carolyn *Leilani* La'au or betah Lalau, someday.

## The Cosmogony of the Pineapple Cannery

Just think! I almost whited-out the turning point in my Little Lulu Lau life: the cannery. How many of you ever worked in a *cannery*? I asked my former deskmate, the writer Willyce Kim, if she ever worked in Gertrude Stein's *there* and after chuckling, her delayed response was, "the cannery? The cannery? No, I had allergies and dermatitis. No." My own rich gang-friends will not believe that snobby Carolyn Lau ever worked in sucha low-class hellhole but in the temp(orary) tradition of my grandmother and mother, I aspired. I ascended, I processed. I quit.

—My husband quizzed if I had signed on for the money and, insulted, I defended, "No." Everybody *else* wanted a job including my cousin Bonnie who was my age. Serendipitously (wow, whata big word; almost like "philanthropic." Hard to say if no mo) serendipitously, my boyfriend and I were scheming to set up Bonnie and Walter: scouting for a job seemed an ideal way to impose the two together. I, Karyle Lau, socialite extraordinaire, imagined that I was *only* "acting out" job-hunting and was *only* to be in the car as a theater prop. Out for a ride, *maybe something interesting could happen that day*; but me, land a job? Historically, I supported summer school, the Art Academy, or perhaps once, the YWCA. Nonetheless, I dressed down like Lucille Ball as if she were pretending to enter the job force, because a *job*, at the pineapple cannery—book monster as I was—impossible! How dare I work—*in the cannery*! Even while filling out the form—I thought it was improvisation or *something*. "Imagining" a job at the cannery was within comprehension, but "having" a cannery position, actually toiling among aliens—Who desired a *cannery* job? Maybe something like Moon Goddess Princess greeting people at the governor's mansion or some Liberty House with pantyhose and nail polish robot but not the cannery.

Shock, denial, genuine nightmare is how I felt when the lady grinded out "Report to work tomorrow" in the pidgin tone, go-to-hell enthusiasm. While it is my habit to analyze a situation which appears irrational, I now realize that at that moment, I embraced Language Poetry. Cause and effect objectified and properly stated, there was nothing I could squeak out to alter the course. Bonnie landed a *job and* was happy. The fellas were bummed because they weren't hiring that day. I possessed a position that I didn't want, need, love, expect and presumably would embrace the next day! Bonnie was a worst hothouse flower than I, what was she anticipating by working in the cannery?

So, my husband sez, "Didn't do it for the money?" The outrage! I succumbed because sybarite me failed to register for summer school. Properly, I was dreaming milktoast summer songs: getting pregnant; flashing that four-carat diamond ring and buying buying buying at Ala Moana. Get bored, raise hell; blast the air conditioner and cruise for advanced shopping or lunch at the Carole & Mary fashion show at the Royal Hawaiian. Eat that fat fat *ono* macadamia(n) nut pie. Gossip about the same old stories and be coupled with a guy identical to me. Of course, none of the above happened: we never honeymooned through the summer. Reynold offered himself to someone more of the nail-having-been-hit-on-the-head-and-adjusted type. As for me, I starred in a new life. Walking and strategizing on my own feet neither capable of swimming nor riding a bike because the parents protected me, protected me. Private school scholar, restricted from association with any low class, I commenced upon my fast-track career in the cannery, and I loved it.

Now, I will expand and enrich your lives and invite you Inside the cannery. First of all, you know you're involved in "the beyond" that has no reference to prior experience. The "environment" is blitzkrieg overdose. Camus would crack up in an instant. Nietzsche *probably* couldn't hang either. Ideally, Blakean: an invigorating twenty-four-hour sidewalk sale of pineapple slop leaking from little cans whizzing above your head as you proudly run to your table with hordes of idealists. Sometimes, the tray boys bang you with a full load of trays stacked with yellow fibrous acid just for fun. Heh heh, bettah laugh and swear "Aye, you like chance?" Or, they will continue to bruise your psyche until you cordially return a *lei* of "No thank you, pig's ass."

You wear a white clown hat if you are a packer or trimmer. The *haole luna*, the white foremen, look like Mormons trying to convert you to working harder. Lugging around those tally sheets, their nervous eyes under pointy felt hats. Those pencils always writing writing writing on that hardtack clipboard. When they weren't writing, their arms were like arrows pointing to that section; those cans; why was this table not running? Always ordering, never cracking a smile. Sometimes, they were running and everybody in the cannery transformed into the waters of the Red Sea for the white *luna*. And, everybody was hoping that he wouldn't slip on some eensy pimple of pineapple. And the rest of the everybody hoped he would and sizzle in the pineapple juice. But the other *luna* were great. They stole pineapple for you. Inevitably, somebody in their family was married to somebody in your family. They wore green hardhats or soldier hats. Some were mechanic foremen. Some were in charge of containers. Only the *haole* could be in charge of Operations. (we all know dat)

The din of tins being crashed *l'un* upon *l'autre*, slamming on the scales as they are being weighed; *les petits* trucks racing in the background lifting pallets of gallon cans to be blasted out into the universe or impounded; the same humpty-dumpty songs returning on the loudspeaker—those hideous boys and their gravy smiles who tried to make time with a careerest like myself and the overwhelming fear of the unknown: people talking loud. My family never talked loud. People clucking and quacking, licking, and mooing in all sorts of sounds and bodies and colors. There were lots of Samoans, Hawaiians, Part Hawaiians, Portagees of course, Filipinos, mix of Chinese, Japanese, and I guess, Koreans. No Blacks; one or two rare stand-up comic whites. I suspect it was the real world. Never permitted to venture beyond the family compound, never allowed to cross a street by myself until I was in the sixth grade, I never knew anyone except my family. Correction: I never knew anyone had face/class except my family. Everyone, everything else was a part of the maze, the din: congestion. And beyond my paper sketches, theories, and books, I had no clue that these humans, the lightning passions—this tender patience that occasionally lifts its eyebrows to italicize a remark—existed, thrived, actually gave a damn about me.

**The First Day**. The first day my mother supplies me with a brown paper bag with a warm ham and green onion omelet sandwich and one dollar because "You need to eat. You're too skinny. It's hard work. You need some nourishment. Be sure to eat something during your break, too."

What madness was this? What sort of appetite did she anticipate I would develop under the electric chair of my current profession? En route, Bonnie jumping out of her skin with delight, her mother Aunty Mabel began to caution us about the pineapple acid and make sure that our gloves were Always DRY.

While her bingcherry eyes contorted and trapezed, introducing new faces, new samples of terror, Aunty Mapela warned,

"Watch out for dose 'kinds people' who look like dis. Watch out for the tough types. (The eyeballs somersaulting, of course, she meant *māhū*.)

"Stay outa their way and Find out Who the nice foreladies are. Stick wit 'em. Make good. Be nice and good luck."

This was our cannery language pep talk. Aunty Mabel never mentioned "having fun." Fun and activity must be an American concept. With that in mind, my cousin accepted the blessing and felt confident. As for me, I was absorbed by an intense anxiety attack. What were we getting into? How come I had no prior orientation and opportunity to ask questions? Who? What? Where? When? Why? My Bill of Rights. The Fundamental Constitution of Good English. No matter that I had never played doctor or cannery before, or how suspicious I was, we were there. The end.

I always regret the fact that I have never had a job as a waitress, but if waitressing is anything near to my career as a packer, my fascinations may just be a lump of wet *kūkae.*

A: I looked stupid: therefore, I had an indignant image on my shoulder—currently referred to as "attitude." Those man-sized used-by-everyone gloves reeked of leprosy. Some people purchased their own gloves, tools of the profession. And they pronounced my name funny—so, so pidgin: "Ca-lyn," with emphasis on the first syllable instead of a roll that culminates in a presence of adagio, Which is how my family pronounces it. Hawaii, Hawai'i—*kapakahi kapakahi.* Nuts, man.

It took me one day of not becoming the piston in a pump. I could not and was not interested in determining Fancy from Choice pineapples, blemish from crush. Without warning, the table would evolve into a born-again feast of time and-a-half speed while juicy clumps of pre-sliced cylinders suggested their bodies into my hands slotted for destiny. Bonnie and I closed our conscious hearts and squeezed, smashed, squashed, violated pineapple after pineapple. Sometimes, the forelady would shoulder up like a panther and just show you what a dunce you were by picking up a can *somewhere*, claiming it was Yours, and threaten that You were not Pineapple Packer caliber. The worst were the assistant foreladies. Talk about needy. Talk about an **e**go problem. If they were in the mood of chastising you, never mind dialogue. Those chiefs specialized in Hitler; their angst apparent. The foreladies all displayed the blue band around their fore-heads; the assistant foreladies rated blurred brown, the second class. If you were going to *ho'omalimali* someone, the assistants were ignored. And thus, they insisted upon attention. Middle fingers, they fell through the cracks between head and toe.

People fell in love at the cannery. Couples smooched openly behind a pole. Or petted between stacks of cans. The pineapple birds would carouse in the cafeteria lingering over boxes of *bento* or plates of steamy spaghetti. Workers brought *ukulele(s)* to the cafeteria and would sing delicate Hawaiian tunes between the bands of rock 'n 'roll. Caps and aprons still on, we were once again, briefly who we were prior to our time at the company. They all knew I was smart. They all knew I was stuck-up and "so sheltered." After a few kicks in the egg roll, even I knew I was stuck-up. After ignoring the advice of my impatient mother, I took her suggestion of learning the art of kissing the glutinous butt of my forelady. My mother sent our famous pirie mangoes to her through me—and I became an instant insider. Having been a worker herself, my mother realized these necessary bribes were my calling card to local custom. And it proved another point among the many that Mildred has imprinted into my thick constipated head: people are *tres simple*.

Don't try to make sense to folks with ideas in real life. Give gifts. If you can give money, that's even more impressive. And boy, was Masako scary looking with her teensy-weensy eyes, elephantine buck teeth, facial expressions careening pathos and wrath and, of course, fat. She did have the most amazingly soft *dofu* hands. And tough as she was, she thought I was funny. She even could see, I could be nice. And when she laughed, she always hid her Dracula teeth. Because, she was really shy underneath her command of quality control. Fat and shy. I used to be skinny. Sometimes still I am shy. Generally, I am suspicious but I am pretty local in that I am enjoying my fat.

Everybody, everybody in Hawai'i is *momona*—c'mon. Only de *haole* stay jogging/sweating and enjoying the beating of that hot hot sun. Not me, not my family.

## The Inner Life of Lani Moo

This is one touchy subject that I cannot objectify. To some folks, "Lani Moo" is merely a matter of phonemes, an abstraction at best. A sound perhaps. Others might confuse Lani Moo with *mu'umu'u*. The go-aheaders consider Lani a relic, a thing of the past to forget. Then, there are the In-betweeners who along with shortie and Suzy *mu'umu'u*; beer-can hats, handmade cloth book covers and slippers, desk calendars with thermometers; going down to Aloha Tower to throw streamers and confetti, leis and money into the water for the divers as the Lurline and Mariposa drifted into fantasyland—the In-betweeners remember. An then, like Elvis fans dead and alive, there are the *pa'a* toughnuts, the underground killerbees *others* like me who derive nirvana from the concept, the riddle and memory of, ice cream parties; the at-Halloween-only chocolate molds of witches and cats and orange custard half-moons and pumpkins packed in break-your-teeth dry ice that you couldn't breathe the same way Aunty Scan instructed when you drove past the mental institution down in Kaneohe— because you could get dumb or crazy like dem. For kids in Hawai'i who hate hate hate stinky smelly toejam cheese, the way the family tells it, it was the brainstorm of my uncle Tong Lee, father of Nelia Beatrice Stanley Flossie and Jimmy; husband of Tai Yi—innovator, he created Lani Moo for Dairyman's because island kids like myself liked only to squish the cheese between the holes in swiss cheese. In those days (as we refer to) only the *haole* ate cheese. The *avant-garde* Lee's were the only relatives who had cheese in their ice box. Locals did not eat cheese—we had much mo bettah food to eat.

We whacked-up *saimin,* portuguese sausage, *kim chee, lomi lomi* salmon, *pipi kaula.* Our beloved *poi* and orgasmic rice. Rice with *lup cheong;* rice with egg omelet; rice with canned corned beef and onions. Yummm. Sometimes, after we eat a whole dinner, we eat rice and tea. *Ono,* so good. And, we'd fight for the burnt rice at the bottom of the pot (you need a pot for this and actually, this is not supposed to happen unless you are yakking on the telephone or maybe you fell asleep waiting to turn off the stove in time to avoid having burnt rice). Cheese was like pok and beans—something that only *haole* ate. Proudly, we ate meat. Man, we ate with straight backs/we spoke English. Just like my China husband sez when he describes himself in ESL terms as "the best speaker of English"—we celebrated diagramming sentences. Who needed to eat cheese on top of that! And who could suffer and bury your taste buds in that ugly white pus-sy stuff: milk? You know, Hawaiians know how—to Eat.

But it wasn't eating that my class stayed in for recess too many lectures while I knew it was not me that threw in that whole baby-size container of milk into the rubbish can. I hated that white uky stuff. It looked ugly and didn't taste like food. No God, no Miss Whiteface could force me to suck that warm sour "cow milk" during those wet hot days. I don't care if we had graham crackers or crack—I did not and would not drink that thick white medicine. That white drink. That poison. Enter Lani Moo.

Lani—Moo. Remember Lani—moo?

Lani Moo was sacred. She was her own unique version of the sacred Hindi cow, sexy as hell. Cue-tte! Children of the unborn children, *kupuna*, Aunty Lani Moo, *hula* maiden, *tūtū*. Nymph: Lani Moo was centerfold. Just saying the sounds, "Lani" swept me to the heavens where all the *aloha* in the world comes from. Not the classic long Hawaiian name. Lani Moo was *kaona* itself. She is truly revered as our Mother Teresa, our Madonna, Madame Curie, Wonder Woman. Drop dead when you say her name. She was libidinous James Bond in a formidable shape. And the "Moo" piece was genuinely the mystical, meditative, and lovestruck part of Lani's awesome symbolism. Loved by plants and animals; heads of state, past and future. Regaled higher than all *ali'i* and gods, included in the *Kumulipo* creation prayers, Lani Moo with her fresh carnation and plumeria leis internally pumping iron while posing along Kalaniana'ole Hwy in grass. Never ever even laid cowslop while kids stood in line dazed by headache heat desiring to touch her forehead. Patient. Understanding: caressing our pitiful hearts with soothing vowels while forgiving our broken English as we honored her in our island simple manners.

Anthropomorphic that she was, briefly, we had meaning in our disenfranchised lives.

And then, there was the matter of Lani's baby. Hawaiians are crazy about babies. Baby anythings are cute. To us, babies mean chance. Maybe change, but hopefully a chance for change. Every baby born is potentially a Kawaipuna or Pono or Maile or Iwalani or Owana or Moke or Nainoa or Kalanihiapo: every baby born is influenced by passion for that *'āina*. The little *keiki* moo was important in the genealogy but Who remembers the name? Who cared if there was a bull or not? That nut Calvin/Kaleo quipped, "Immaculate Conception Moo, right?" All that mattered was the Unmoved Mover Lani Moo. Sensitive nostrils, galaxy big eyes, vamp orange-brown and white *kīkepa* wrapped around her *'ōpū*. One *wahine* woman, female, mother, island girl, sex. No flies. Never any flies around Ms. Moo. She was an identity: no lunch cans or plastic icons dared replicate her bestial beauty. A milkcover maybe which entitled you to a Lani Moo ice cream feast day where you could get free ice cream, all the milk (urrgh) and cheese (aarph) you wanted, and schmooze with Lani Moo for a second. If politicians ever learn the secret of Lani Moo, we will be in good or bad *kūkae* aka shit!

Then, Lani went *holo holo. Pau hana.*

P.S. An den: you know what went happening now! Pogs! Yea, what the hell are *pogs*? Metal replacements for the unique cardboard caps that held the cream and milk together—pogs that cost individually from fifty or one hundred dollars which are now used as gambling chips! The New Hawaiian rave sweeping kids, the super markets, *obachan*, and P.R. men into the latest "Go for Broke" mindset, pogs. The ugliest.

The dumbest of the dumb and yet, it is the rage: almost as high as each crane layering on the steel or thick as the layers of cement that protect it. Cann you replace Lani Moo with tofutti? Could you replace milk cover with metal?

*Auē koʻu Hawaiiʻi Nei!*

## The Presence of Lite Spam-lingering in my psyche for a long time but oozing out after the (first) Rodney King verdict.

Anyone who is a darky—that is "who lives inside light- or dark-colored skin," poor or both—has eaten the forerunner of *pate*, spam. I wonder how the buggah's name "spam" was born? "Ham" in the "spa"? "Spit" plus "ham"? "the Sp(irit) in the present tense of the verb 'to be,'" communing in the "am"? Or was it just military *cordon bleu cuisine*?

With the advent of Yuppies in Hawaiʻi, a competition was devised among local wannabe yuppies to contest in a spam-diversity competition. Spam *pate*, spam *musubi* (a kind of *sushi*), and delicious rewarding fresh from the can with jelly and cold white lard probably horse meat and flyswappings in the spam staring *and* yuckking-it-up-at-you-in-the-face Third World Spam hands down authentic turn the silver key attached to the can spam incarnate gospel finally becomes Legitimate. The poet sculptor painter activist gardener husband father cook visionaire jokester Imaikalani warned me about his now famous spam stew. Cringing, I begged, "What the hell you put in it?"

"A lot of potatoes, man!" he smacked.

Those "damn spam" sushi/musubi are enthusiastically bought and sold at every honorable *sushi* stand at home in Kaleponi where everybody, everybody, is calesterol-conscious. At every Hawaiian event, there are the food booths with, of cuss, spam. In 1992, Lite Spam appears first in paper—literature: always the first art to be eliminated—becomes the prize introductory media to premier Lite Spam followed by discretionary late night tv ads. What can this mean to a Naive Native? Aye! what's happening to us now? This is an example of deep counter-culture adverse manipulation assimilation *buffet a la carte* in our butts. This lite spam is the new tool for exchange brokerage—the new nails. After a flash of *hā* and *ʻōlelo* word power, I race to the telephone and dial 808. Know what that is? The area code to Hawai'i, man. In trouble, dial 808. On the coconut wireless, I shout the scandal to my chiefs of culture.

We are burned up, mostly we suffer from a kind of ancient pain: (You know Lololo? Tita—One. Da Screamer rattled our McInerny three-piece vested brains and Hawai'i Visitors Bureau Hawaiian Telephone operator voices. That Ph.D. said that Someting wass wrong.—I dunno if SHE got da ANSA though.)

Da tightshoe Madison Avenue execs (all kine color) who sell our land, our weather, and get on the plane to lū'au in our backyard ain't factoring in the brahhss and sisstahs who put our big feet inside-out college departing with the palapala—before and after Civil Rights. No matter, mainstream-kind-scared American—Japan too—no gettum darkies: akamai—hip to double- and triple-talk hardcopy assessment deadline net worth. Some of us are white, some of us be village green. We have learned from Chinese to conquer people by marriage. Give you the best singing and sex in your no mo fun lives. Aye Progressive, because we only in our developmental stages of processing bureaucratic white agenda and underneath it all, somewhere, yes sir, yess ma'am, we not logic by your instruments of measure. Some white folks, as much as we love you and you may have children by us: we nevah expect you and intelligent converted colored—yellow, red brown, sage, indigo, florida Hawaiian folks nevah know that we no get the verbs "to be" or "to have" in our wishes.

Means, we no lik compete an cut troat for success. 'a'ole, NO.

Who asked Captain Cook come Hawai'i an insult us into Victorian habits and uniforms? You know what follows? Syphilis, false eyelashes, shoes, peanut butter and jelly sandwich, Miss Hawaii contest, Ala Moana Shopping Center. The otta day myfren Ivan the psychiatrist went say in pidgin rhythms, "Man, I have been having angst." Poorting, needed to say it in Nazi talk what he felt as a star trekking kanaka. (The greatest is when I was home and had to report a lost item to who? my favorite, the Honolulu Police.

When the Hertzgirl said that, "All security was involved in something and would be tied up for an hour,"

I said, "What? Somebody was murdered?" The joke did not go over: we all knew the cops were eating dinner and did not want to bother with some tourist who lost something.

Later on, at my mother's, I call the cops and up drives this cute little meter maid cart and in it is a disarming local boy in a cop's costume. When he walks up to the house, I invite him in and he begins to unlace his shoes! Soo cute! [At that moment, I knew someday, I would move home just so that as an "old fut" I could push anyone around. Instead, I offer that he interviews me in the kitchen where he can enter through the back door and therefore leave his shoes on.]) But as far as *kānaka maoli* and our lost kings and queens, before the missionaries and then Mackindly Mckinley screwed us, eh? Thee United States government—man, *haole*: how did Christians learn from their god to be so *mākonā*—so mean. How come *haole* love to hear our music and love to watch us *hula* but never let us—"forbid" was the word; how come *kānaka* were forbidden to *'ōlelo o Hawai'i*—speak Hawaiian. No wonder we real *da kine* and like beef or cry all da time—try-ing to reach our metaphors, man. When we had *ali'i*, we had *ahupua'a*, system. Oh, it was *some system* and Ka'ahuamanu did her share to create even more complexity to it, but bottom line, it was Hawaiian. We had slaves and human sacrifice: it was not humanistic or maybe not even democratic but it was okay. And, along comes the whitebutts to embarrass our people to wear corsets and girdles around our throats. Exercise and Diets! Those English and those damn wigs? And while I'm *nuha*—**what is it with people who need to conquer** people? Talk about an inferiority complex! Must be someting wrong. Whoa, now, after convincing us that our beloved and adopted spam not good for us, what is next? Words: when I was born, my father—disappointed that I wasn't a boy disguised my name to link with Charlemagne. My Hawaiian name is so common that I never used it before my friend Faye made it sound so pretty and sweet. All my life I have had impossible too much heaven in my body for this earth. Maybe because my Chinese and Hawaiian names both have heaven in them. Best thing that I have learned in life is to make a good life here and not worry about heaven. For a while, I changed my Hawaiian name to "Leilo'i," meaning "flowers in the mud terrace." I kept the *lei* part because it was half the name that my daddy gave me. And I *hānai*, adopted the *lo'i* part because that is where *taro*, our staple food, flourishes. That is where the *'ohā*, the old root, and the *kalo*, the first *taro*, growing from the planted stalks and the *keiki*, the new shoots, thrive. In the *lo'i*, the *'ohana*, the entire family of water, insects, mud, wind, salt air; the fish that wander in by accident; the hands that come to gather and plant *taro* within the *'āina*: which we are, belong: meaning. We are meaning. We cry, fight, and love each other. More is nevah enough passion. Sometimes we are like the birds and sometimes we are Pele. We like to go barefeet because in Hawai'i even dirt tastes good. Our earth is *Papa*; our mother, sweet. Our water is sweet and soft. In a way, we are kind of like babies. Maybe that is the shadow side of us as our skin wrinkles slowly—now the cosmetics industry doing test on us wondering how *kupuna* no mo wrinkles. We have a here-and-now kind of nature and that, in comparison to NYSE or NASDAQ, just doesn't cut it.

If you want to come see and have fun, *hele mai*. Come look at us. See if you can find the Indians in the puzzle. See if you can tell we are standing in line behind and before you at the Safeway in your hometown. We will not appear in costume, but just let your heart leak a little sweetness or laughter and we will balloon our *kolohe* bodies. If you go to the source of red dirt, however, please, *kōkua*. Ask first, and then no steal our bones and put your name on top of *the name* of our most loved *kupuna*. No make shame.

It has been long years to figure out how and who and what race and color go good with my skin and ears. And then you have to throw it to the wind like a fisherman throwing the net out to sea. To catch crab, turtles, shoes, a husband, my kids, my bigbest family in the world or nothing. Maybe tears, maybe laughs. And, then after I wrote testimony for *Hoʻokolokolonui*, I changed my name back to Lei-lani and then Lei-lanilau. And then, I made another list of windows to look out or into.

**THE LIST (for today)**

| | |
|---|---|
| The Slop Can Man | The Marriage Proposal in Hawaiian |
| Beatrice's Hernia | My Kona Hat   *Manapua* Man on Bicycle |


## *ʻAumakua*: An Example of Hawaiian Thought Processes

Lately (in the September/October 1992 issue of *Poets & Writers*) "some people" who want to be known as Hawaiian, have been leaking *ʻōlelo* here and there like farts.

The latest in-concept among non-Us, has been the naïve usage of the term *ʻaumakua*. For anyone who seems to imagine "doing Hawaiian" as the new frontier to conquer in translation: warning, **Beware**.

Those of us who are just peeking out of closets to sniff the air cautiously proceed with blessing from our *kupuna*, our *kumu*, or our *ʻaumakua*. Unless you are truly skillful, dedicated, and gifted, no *kupuna* no *kumu*—the master teachers or caretakers of our culture—would accept you as an apprentice.

In the old way, you were <u>selected</u>. Like Kawena Pukui who was *hānai*. Every step of the way, Tested. Pukui was trained, tested. Watched and blessed, tested to be the carrier, voice, the vessel, song of our culture.

You weren't chosen because of your family or you got a grant or because you could imitate *haole* real good; or because you look pretty good or because somebody could pay to be blessed. *ʻAʻole*, no. Not any old body was chosen.

It was not "equitable." Only the best. With good ear power connected to da instinct(s) and with a tongue that rivaled water, birds, fire, wind.

For a while things were completely outa hand in Hawai'i—getting lik dat again—when everybody flying in wanted a piece of title so after being so nice and waiting for the *malahini* to adjust and being so *ho'omanawanui*, so patient, finally, Hawaiians stepped in: *'a'ole*, now you have to be certificated to be particular *kumu* or *kupuna*.

Still, only one Larry Kimura and one *Morning Dew*. Only one Pukui; only one Maile Meyer and Eric Enos. One David Malo.

Nonetheless, for those too impatient to bribe their way into Hawaiian insiders, too disinterested to be possibly rejected, a way to *hānai* (adopt) oneself into the inner sanctum was to create one's own *'aumakua 'ohana*. The problem is that these very folks had no clue as to how fragile and volatile and mostly impractical this gesture was. Most adventurers of this type fail to know the concept of *'aumakua 'ohana* and because in Hawai'i we refer to it simply as *'aumakua*, nouveau voyeur-participants casually refer to "my *'aumakua*" like it is their pet rock. What they don't realize is that one's *'aumakua* has the right to discipline you. Yell at you while you stay in front of da computer and squeeze the "badness" out of you to Ho'oponopono—Get on the right path! I heard about some *haole* guys who had signs of menopause—nightsweats, inside-out vagina, breast that ballooned and exploded just as they were delivering papers at the University of Hawai'i! They *delivered* those papers in pidgin! And then, you heard about the Japan American literati whose fingernails won't stop growing like conveyor belts?

Those of us who grew up with underground *'aumakua* know and expect— hope—that our *'aumākua* **will** guide us. Cannot help (it), they are our ancestors —the combined force of rocks, geckos, sharks, owls—all our ancestors, which is why it is called *'aumākua 'ohana*. **Remember** when I mentioned my Hawaiian *tūtū*? I expect my *tūtū* to straighten me up by me having dreams; or maybe, I'll cry and be moody when it's not simply a matter of PMS. Sometimes, I cannot go somewhere or see certain people because of how the clouds appear or maybe, it could be a matter of the lack or presence of wind. **Remember** when I mentioned my cousin Robert Wilcox, the one that locals refer to as the "Maui Wilcoxes— the poor Wilcoxes. The one that went start the rebellion against annexation." What about my father and my sister? These are my *'aumākua*. No stuffed animal. My father scared the English language outa me and excited the dullness when

I planned to water the backyard one day *while I was just going down the stairs*
behind the outside deck.
You know what! before flying to a stupid nearby plum tree,
a fluff of wind
width of dirt,
an owl
my brown and white and grey feathers daddy was like making my deck *his hale*
on the railing (well, to think like a *kanaka*, I guess it is his too).
Where were the neighbor's kids to show the owl?
Where were my artist and straight friends in the neighborhood?
I called my husband at Walnut Creek. He did not believe me. Then, he
zipped home and he still demanded that it was not true. He shook his head,
businessman as he is, refused to believe that an owl,

my father, was introducing himself to the both of us in the most delicate
intimacy.

Sacred and soft.
Wondrous and revealing a side unknown to anyone else: finally safe to be
Hawaiian.
Sweet and cool under the redwood branches.
My daddy, my daddy!
Anybody who is linked to their *'aumakua* could tell it was my father.
If you saw him, you would say, "Aye Jackie Lau, *pe hea 'oe*?
Howzit?" *Kānaka maoli*—Hawaiians can tell by the way I tell this story (beyond
merely the page), the intelligence of their antennae, ears sculpted to determine
circumstance just by the sound of *hā*—that breath of life and how it is sounding
at the moment. *Hā* and *'ōlelo*, the two most important clues on earth. A
Hawaiian, that is, a practicing twenty-first centurion, is not showing off the
outward signs of *being Hawaiian*. Hattie could be captured with a net and
skewered off to the Smithsonian. A true Hawaiian does not behave like those
HVB hotel hula dancers. Like that nut Imai too. Hawaiians—the classy ones—
never show off and are always nice—like that prince Sonny Palabrica. Even
when they're bad—they never swear because they have so much *kaona*—
metaphoric ways of expressing the appropriate indirect meaning from our litany
of proverbs.—Like that Japan American fake literati I mentioned earlier
he is *Haumanumanu ka ipu 'ino 'ino*:
"A misshapen gourd makes an ugly container."
Instead of calling a human a "fuckup" or "asshole" how about this poetry?

As for me, my *'ohana* refer to me as "the sugar cane that makes the mouth raw when chewed." Home.

What was the logic behind this huge—phantom—owl in our yard?! And it stayed until my younger daughter came home from school. That owl hung around for hours and I was epileptic/tortured and joyous at the same time. Answer: This is a very common example of Hawaiian style *ha'ina 'ia mai ana ka puana*, explaining *'aumakua*: I "have to tell the story like it is." In the past, when I had other experiences and most of my life I ws told I was crazy and believed I was insane. No, it was just my *'aumākua*—good thing I found out!

**When I was a kid, so much *pilikia*,** I had to walk over fire all the time.

It all began when I was a baby because my mother used to hang my diapers out while the funeral procession drove by our house.

When my mother hung the diapers at different hours and finished three days of chanting and carrying me over fire, my belly button stopped bleeding.

Later, I had to do it by myself while my mother and aunty chanted.

Oh I was scared, felt I was being punished because I was stupid.

It was kinda sexual too; like Pele teasing me.

When I had my own kids and they got sick, we just sat by the fire, me watching the colored comics burn to ash with the window open so the bad spirit could fly out and their good one could step in at night before I put them to bed if they needed the treatment.

They never had to walk over fire. That's the difference.

It's going to be longer and harder for them to be part of the tradition.

Everything is so/too rational.

But maybe not, they can separate their ethnic and psychic lives from their public lives: they know how to hide the psychic stuff in ways I don't know. I think the technique is called "deflecting."

And I couldn't go into the ocean because THEY said that the *shark 'aumakua* dreamed for me. So I don't know how to swim. You can imagine what failure I feel like as a common Hawaiian. Little in common except our beloved *'ōlelo*. When we hear our *'ōlelo* we cry and cry and cry. It's our best friend, our therapy which binds us to nature, our mother and father.

Can you imagine, those damn *haole* missionaries! illegally outlawing our beloved words! We sing and dance our *'ōlelo* of magic. Make you just want to make love day and night. *Haole* used to only love to hear us sing the songs night and day. But we have proverbs to work by and it's on the hard drive. And we got girl groups that can really make you cry. Change yourself silly. Ipo can get people to tattoo themselves in the old style of geometric patterns with a bamboo! *Auwē!* Watch out for Ipo's eyebrow that wiggles like ships when she convinces you about whatever Ipo wants.

And before I forget, I gotta mention that there are all kinds and shapes of *'aumākua*. For instance, **if** it is impossible to be in a relationship with anyone, maybe it's because you already mated with your *'aumakua*. You could even be married but have no interest with your partner. Probably you and your *'aumakua* have something happening. This happened to me! I was married. Got divorced. Had boyfriends galore. No, I only was interested in things that were happening in the 10th century. William Blake was my modern interest. So everybody I liked had to be an old soul and I am not attracted to fuds. That was half my life. Enter my husband from an ancient city after years of therapy climaxing with my near suicide. And then the words from Sophie, a nun who taught me how to fold laundry. She said, "Say good-bye to your father and your sister. Tell your father you love him and to stop bothering you. Go to his grave and end it." When I went to his grave, my mother talked to him outloud (I always "thought" to him), and when I was leaving I turned and from my body, unplanned, it was as though Someone else said, "*A hui hou.*" See you later.

It was probably my entire *'aumākua* wishing me *aloha* and hello and protection. And I was so happy, loved, so certain that unless I'm writing a proposal where everybody's so uptight about the format and presentation, the grammar, vocabulary, and diaphragm of Good English, I will continue to live in the vigor of my mother's hometown in Kohala (with my *'aumākua*) guided by this *'ōlelo no'eau*:

*He pa'ā kō kea no Kohala, e
kole ai ka waha ke 'ai.*

"A resistant white sugar cane of Kohala which can make the mouth raw when chewed."

*I mua!*

## From Latin to Latino; from *Nopales* to *Panini*

In between writing non-paying articles; reading nearly as much Hawaiian history as I did Chinese history (and at my age starting all over again is like having sextuplets); in between begging for justice and hanging with my Oaktown homies (*imua* Oaktown!), I have to get this *kiawe*/mesquite (you noticed? I only italicized the Hawaiian part of the slashed concept because "mesquite")
is probably really "mosquito" or
"mescalito"; "mescara" or "mexicana" but "mesquite"?
Messs-keet—I hear shooting, I feel that horizontal anal verging on Southwest minimalism which hardly *sounds* ethnic.
Mesquite/esthete: no humidity, no loose muscles in my mouth.

> No cushion between my ankles and feet.
> No water under my eyebrows.
> No dirt in my pores.
> *'Āina* says, "Cannot be our *'ōlelo.*" But maybe before it was BMW-ized
> by the yups, maybe it is deep down darkness and therefore, *colored.*

(as I was beginning about breaktime) . . . I have to set the relatives straight on this tradition of macadamia(n) nuts: round cylinder cans which remind me of the cannery, clusters, chocolate, cream pie mess. **Please don't send any more macadamia(n) nuts home to, with, or for me!**
Everytime. Everyvisit. Everybody—there is *Somebody* who bought some *on special*. Wrapped in thick cardboard, in the mail, or suitcases along with guava or passion fruit juice, non-stop flights of macadamia(n) nuts arriving and stored in the pantry. "Oh, no, more of those 'gawddamn' nuts," the Little-Getting-Big daughter sez.

The other daughter just bats her eyelashes in philosophic acceptance of the larger system, the uninterrupted order of family ritual. On the other hand, if you were a family member AND <u>didn't</u> (after all these lifetimes) send, give, plague us with those nutty bombs
I wouldn't be normal.
I'd be doubting my worth and disappointedly hurt.
I never eat those things.
"Your neighbors will love it!" says my mother the Red Hen.

"Give some to the lady that drives Ana to school."
You never know when you have to shove a box or can in someone's face while smiling and mention that
"These just arrived from Hawai'i. Enjoy."
I used to like the unsalted kind so I could make that killer macadamia(n) nut fatso pimples and so so flaky crust pie. Now, I don't dare become excited about the idea. But I can hardly wait to go home and eat one! Uuuuhh . . . As a matter of fact, I'll admit that after complaining and lecturing about these nuts to my mother's face And informed her that I was going to write about it, she says
"They're on sale at Long's for $2.99."
"Let's go," I said.


But *kiawe* is something I can smell and want to burn in my fireplace—why not??? It smells so *ono*. Here on mainland, you got that potpourri crap sold everywhere from Payless to boutiques for every occasion in every place.
I like burn some in my fireplace on a cold day or rainy night—I'm goin be the *pua'a*, the sacrificial *lū'au* pig.
You can eat me if I am cooked.
I will probably taste yummy. I have been enjoyed by most people most of my life, why wouldn't I taste delicious cooked?
I don't have to barbeque *something* just so that I can smell a combination of Hanauma Bay and fantasize one oversized pig—daddy ripping the crunchy greasy skin off for me. Some people burn incense; I like burning chunks of *kiawe*. Maybe, some days I'll just burn some *kiawe* for the flavor in the air. When you grow up in the islands, you are really horny for smells all the time because everywhere, there is the salt air and maybe your aunty is drying some salted fish or meat in the backyard. You also got those flowers making you allergic to "purified air." I mean, your dreams are interfered with that ginger outside squeezing itself between your nostrils and your neurons. All my dreams have been forever altered because of that early childhood socializing with the plants and animals. And everywhere you go, *plumeria*.
And my family is so arrogant: we no mo *kālā*, but we get bambula-size *pīkake*. Everybody comes to beg or steal our *pīkake*. Some people get big- size diamonds; our *pīkake* big like potatoes.


When my mother was in labor with me and she had me by C-section in the middle of a tidalwave the day before April Fools'
my daddy went hatchet the biggest *pīkake* that he and my uncles could load into

the truck. Then they went drive the truck to the hospital that had no anesthesia that day
and daddy held ma's hand while the doctor cut
with that *pīkake* drowning out everybody's *pilikia*.
That's how I came into Kapi'olani Hospital. That's why I gotta have smells but mesquite, non; *kiawe, si, si*

## Application—Another one (thank god, or do I mean, oh fuck?)

I'm applying for a job now.—Not so high mucky-muck but according to the ad, I'm not *qualified* because I'm not *eligible*. (Will that stop the cousin to Kalanihiapo? Hell no.)

When you're invisible
when your mother tongue was—I don't even have the finest most accurate words only the
tears, screams, scars
when you have been a professional writer for twenty-odd years creating a "career" in a
foreign language in a foreign style because you had no clue,
no clue that your perfect/imperfect *'ōlelo* was outlawed in its own land

you feel like you're a misttake.
Something that was overlooked in the final printout and

you're THere for sure but the intention was that
you should have been deleted.

I like sue the US government for all the thousands of dollars I spent in therapy, alcohol, and drugs to numb the pain; to reason out why I feel like a freak (cannot though because *kanaka* iss wards of the state and wen da *haole* wen write da laws fo Hawai'i to become annexed, guess what? we too stuupit to know wass good fo us eh? )

I think; therefore, I freak

Who has the right to take somebody's belief system, sounds, wet kisses and hugs, teasing, *'aumakua* away from not just one, but an entire population? And then, we have to not only write white grammar and spelling. In order to be successful in anyting, you gotta live, feel it—*maybe* even marry and have kids by It.

Man I am bored and confused and disgusted by English. Is this not the twin thing that happened to the Indians? Don't people get sued because of the environmental abuse or child abuse or harassment?
Q: How come the US government can get away with dis?
Hypothesis: maybe da military like the beaches, like da hosspitality we know
          how give.
          maybe da militay like da view, da wehda and *ono* kine food

The difference between Andrew and 'Iniki is that Andrew is *haole* name and here on the continent—far from, far from "paradise" and 'Iniki, "to pinch, nip; sharp and piercing, as wind or pangs of love"—iss too romantic. So when two hurricanes hit at about the same time and Kaua'i was whipped and almost wiped out, how come, on the news, you always hear about the "victims of the hurricane"—and I am expecting to see somebody I know on television—my cousin fixing something or some Hawaiian sounds or pidgin accent. Nahting. Not even a "dirty rat" politician that my Hawaiian gang and me could shout, "Aye did you see Ben or Waihe'e on the news?" Nah-Ting. Who cares about the Somalians, the Serbs and Croatians? The Chinese and "humanitarian efforts" should do lunch. *Haole* power: to vacation and control lives in Hawai'i but, no *kōkua* us.

*What is the problem?*
Are we slaves of entertainment?
Slaves of fantasy?
Are we to scaaaared or too nice to confront?
Is the *'āina* so paradise that it is a matter of *puella*—the beautiful woman that you want to be young forever, a pleasing voice, large breasts, sweet milk serving any of your imaginations? Patient, mysterious, no mo mouth, no mo stink eye, no feelings!
I hate that damn Michner. I hate Charlton Heston. That home-boy Elvis: cute, sex; shake his hips like Tahitian dancers—good-intending but not-so-in-Hawaiian-history—Elvis gave us that stupid concrete boat out there in the water. How come *kānaka maoli* never sue the navy for that famous oil still leaking from the Arizona? Get the corrosive wreck and dead *haole* outa our water! We

like sue the navy but cannot because stay Government. Look at the Valdez? Or the Tailhook Party and More—What's the difference?

# What, we Hawaiians stay dumb?

When you go to my hometown, you gonna hear it more and more.
Or maybe the service will be just a little slow.
Or maybe you might find a rat in your pillowcase.

Or when you go deep-sea marlin fishing on the Kona coast and imagine that you are going to a *haole*-style birthday party where you get a toy in the end: you not going catch no fish. Unh-Unh.
You can logic out: how *haole* control that cottage industry going let another dumb *haole* get the local *haole* bread and butter? "Keep his feet to the fire," said the skipper. "Aye, aye," agreed the *haole* on the cellular phone during rush hour traffic in Los Angeles.

I'm sending my portfolio to Sixty Minutes and Prime Time. They never put nothing on their show about January 17, 1993. Sam Donaldson did something on the tobacco industry the other night. And son of a gun, *if* whenever he said "tobacco industry" I didn't translate *that* into "sugar plantation owners." When you work on translations, that kind of automatic shift happens. That's why me and my husband like have these mental orgasms when we "translate" English or Chinese or American or Hawaiian or behavior or situations from language to language. He did proudly acknowledge that he was **marginal**. Me too, me too!

> When your vocab and life experiences take you beyond language, movies, adventures, Little Pleasure, you have reached multicultural multi-ethnic crack-up.

If you can still drive a car and arrive to work on time and even contribute, you deserve a long hug and sloppy Hawaiian wet kiss!

When I saw my friend Travis yesterday, he showed me yet another piece of bullchips.
I said, "Don't you get it? the Quincentennial's over, man."
Behind his thick glasses, my long-winded Papago pal responded,
"You guys are next in line."
"Man, don't you do any work for this city?" I teased.

Travis smiled: intellectual/activists—not know-it-all academic scared cats—spend hours dancing around the fires of our pain; hours writing the words of justice for all. We have pitiful moments left for imagination and creativity because we are always writing to ensure that policy truly is *ho'oponopono*—the right path, not war path.

I looked at Travis and succumbed:

"I hate this waste-time shit. When are those *others* gonna get it?"

As expected, he shrugged.

**(inspired by Wiggenstein)**

The word for that is *ho'omanawa nui*. When you say that, white folks will no longer need to "pursue" ethnicity. Maybe every culture broker will have been booted out so that appropriating will not only be a sin but a thing of the past. Maybe.

When I have all—or at least enough of—my *'ōlelo* back, by the time the words return to my *mana'o*, the *mana* will truly be in place.

No more turtlenecks, neckties, or even expensive soft Italian shoes.

*'Okina* and *kahakō* gonna virus out every other virus.

Finally, there will be *pono*—or at least *kolohe* in every task, every wiggle, every sound.

No more stink eye.

The ocean will come in and out my body.

The meaning of *ahupua'a* will be respected (vertical and horizontal sexland bondage!).

The *lo'i* is planted.

When you go to Hawai'i next time, go to Wai'anae.
If you are trusted, you will be taken to the *lo'i*.
When you come from slime and enjoy it, life is always good.

Aye, brahh, aye sista the revolution-party is in full swing Hawaiian style. You gonna start seeing and hearing real Hawaiians. Remember what young Bob

Dylan said, "Get out of the road if you can't lend a hand." Don't you know the words? Maybe you never listened or forgot?

Who knows what's gonna happen now that I've come into my real *mana*. All us *kānaka*, light-skinned, dark, *momona*, old, *keiki*, office workers, and *kahuna*, we will cast the first stone and catch and play with it. We will honor our *pōhaku* and carve even more gods but no more, no more *pilikia*.

# *Kani ka pila* not *pilikia*.

*Aloha 'āina!*
*Mālama 'āina!*

## Passing

I didn't know—that is never thought about—what this meant until this spring when Haolelani mentioned that she "passed for white."

You know that "all of the sudden feeling"
years of crying Combined with self-hate
repeated days of blame or responsibility for the failure of something in an entire race that goes wrong
No matter how much you attend and guard it from destroying you again?
Son of a gun And then
you feel bad again?
Maybe, nobody knows this feeling.
I know the *haole*—especially the therapists will claim that these signs could apply to anyone.
*Maybe* it is my own.
But everybody who passes for something else knows this Original Sin:
the school principal who is not your pal but the calasssic self-serving schmoozez;
the nurse whose nightingale voice sounds good to her cronies but will not think twice about stabbing you a few times in back with the scissors and when you are gasping,
a few extra hits in the face seem thorough.
She is the loudest mouth new riche who namedrops brands and trends of the moment with no hint of "less is more."
He is the good friend who borrows your savings because of a life or death matter and you end up without your house because it is partytime and You R history.

It is your best friend who wears the sweatshirt your daughter gave you when she went to college because your friend thinks it's "interesting" that she is wearing your clothes for a year while you wait for your turn.

"Passing" is the organization that promotes and advertises in the paper and the mission statement that reflects diversity and multiculturalism *and* has the all-white board.

It can also be the reverse black white hispanic asian combo sandwich writing and speaking and behaving in Passing-for-White through generic ethnic skins. A friend (whom I won't name) commanded, "We need a person of color in a position of authority." The person that he was referring to was a dumbbell and not just a dumbbell, a Thoroughbred Dumbbell kindly known as incompetent so I said,

"So and so cannot do math. He cannot manage a budget of $500. This organization is sinking and you want color?!"

When you know all kinds of colors, ages, types, and you know there are good folks

*Others*, safely you can say,

"Dumb is dumb. Nice is nice."

There are mean dumb disabled people—I know at least one. There are cutthroat whites blacks priests psychiatrists. Don't be fooled by skin or profession. Use your nose to smell out the item. Could it be the Executive Director who has the market on smiling and short on soul?

My own guys two—both passed for altar boys or princes or the boy you'd like your daughter to marry, but they were vampires. My Great Love is getting better some days.

The worst in "passing" is the moment of discovering that **Y**ou yourself

**r**eading the page at this very moment

have been **enjoy**ing the ti **T** le    of passing for something.

When I finally discovered that I pass for Chinese and also knew a little about behaving Chinese—I felt so relieved
that after years of testing myself as though everything was an SAT
And I had to be sure about not selecting the incorrect multi-choice;
therefore, after selecting an answer, I always deliberate on other possibilities (the insider's aptitude philosophy test) then begin worrying that *perhaps*, I didn't consider the details . . . and I don't have to finish this sentence.

# I'm inside out Hawaiian.

I hate cold weather.
I grew up with those mynah birds and orchids in my way. But I need it.
Nuisance is the fragrance of too many plumerias. But I like it.
I am really (rrrhhRreallllleeee—eehaaH) Hawaiian
and was conditioned to be too ashamed that I had dark spooky and wild blood
in me.

I pass for a woman but am really an owl-shark.

For the years of ballet, mentorship with the poets Jack and Stan; after I tried to
follow orders as a wife, I am untrainable
I
Am
UN-TRAIN-ABLE

The 'aumākua in me is too strong. "Electromagnetic fields, explained my friend
Jeffrey/Thomas. Even that bubble Ishmael Reed who looked like a snowman
with headphones on the corner of Haste and Telegraph blew, "Carolyn Lau, you
are too strong." I am not so strong. My guy claimed that he could destroy or
make me happy in a muscle of a thought. It frightened me that he needed to
believe that.
"What gangster movie does he think he's in?" smirked Tom Cookies. A comedy
in passing, I guess.

## The Myth of Pooh-nah-ho

People who went to Punahou like to whirl around the sound as if that bald-
headed Pope himself was a classmate. Pooh Nah Ho ho. Phew No ho as in your
you-know-what.

The people who didn't go to Puh-nah-hoe hate the ones who went there—or
pity them.

Worst than penis envy however is the "Punahou envy," which evolved, developed,
camouflaged is called "agenda."

These burning embers (aka) characterisics include trying to get in as if it is MENSA or the Oahu Country Club or the Pacific Country Club. It's *the* place to become a successful *haole*-in- attitude So? Like everyone who went there is good, smart, and cute? Wrong. Tom Cruise, Gabby Pahinui, and Connie Chung did not go to Punahou. President Clinton never go Punahou—although he probably would have been scholarship type. Kamehameha nevah go Punahou. Bill Gates, Madonna, Stephen Hawking, William Blake never considered Punahou. Rosie Perez, Pholan Devi, Chairman Mao did not attend Punahou. Imelda Marcos applied to Punahou on the back of a matchbook and was rejected. Andrew Young was recruited and declined Punahou though it's an outside possibility that Colin Powell may have attended Summer School.

I went to Punahou and flunked out because I read only what I wanted to read and did not do math at all.

Oh, I kept up in style and then

ka-put = failure. Historic shame.

"She flunked out of Punahou. Shhh."

"Her mother will kill that idiot if she tells this story. Isn't she ashamed of *anything*? Truth is one thing, but doesn't she know how dumb she is? Poor Mildred."

"I feel good," goes the song. Thank god, I have no hang-ups about that.

I was a beautiful kid. Smart—maybe smart-mouthed. Smart-assed—still smart-assed and not only that "too smart-assed avec wrinkles."


QUESTION: do you think it is attractive to be smart-assed or not? a) what if you're kinda cute? b) what if you're kinda funny And nice?


You know, the poet: always speaking in metaphors.

Always "seeing" too clearly. Willful dreamer.

All my life—I wasn't supposed to but I did—go barefeet. Formative years of barefeet while I was breaking the thermometer and tasting that fire-bitter cherry juice.

Barefeet when I stepped into those overripe figs in my father's backyard.

Barefeet when I drive in the summer—who can drive with shoes!? Early and now and still,

reckless days. Erotic afternoons in the lichee tree. Days of raw salmon and seaweed.


Everyday, a ripening of *something*: cheeks, tongue; more tongue and some *ono* cheeks.

Fingers always in and out of mischief. In and out of that red mud; in and out that juicy dirt.

Play with dirt every afternoon. You had to stretch your nostrils so that every sound hallowed its way from the throat to the ego to the right moments and never relax because we always had to measure ourselves with the blondes and blue-eyed manners.
Nonetheless, I really imagined I was something out of this world having based myself on the tampax girls with blue eyes, blue black hair, and fuchsia lips.
In Hawai'i, Crazy know Crazy: once I was in a play and I had to be Sister Saint Somebody and when the directions (came from God of course) that I had to have this "look"
in my eyes, I pasted the blue-black inky look in my eyes and right away! the teacha said
"That's it. Keep it up"

So what about Punahou?
It's an institution where people need/have attitude and aggression to survive. It is definitely Not *Kanaka*; more than Kamehameaha, it means "new spring," but you already know what haappens when the *haole* translates a non-*haole* concept into *haole*.
Pretty ssoon gotta have cement
next thing you know, need aasphalt:
now, get trustees but no mo new springs. Da springs all junk; al broken, get pipes and filtration but no more jump in the sweet water. *Pau*, no more: the baby *wai*, the infant water, the source and essence of *punahou* which is *puna wai*, "spring water." NO MOA

So what?
You gotta be snickering when somebody from the mainland says, "she went to Poon-nah-hoh." Or, "I think his father went to see Punaho." When you are too old to go Punahoa, it is never too late; you can always come back and teach and Puna-hope. Or, you can sen yo kids go Punahopeless. Religious, in the killed or be-killed sense of insecurity: Missionary. Greed. Money. Overkill, a perverse marriage of spirituality and conquest: factory for future *luna*. Symbol of *someting* by association. A matter of successful colon ization. Whew! I never made it. Thank my *'aumākua*. I am really slime and proud of it. That's what happens when you're part shark.

Kathleen Alcalá wrote to me and quipped, "Maybe, your parents were afraid that rather than eating you, the sharks planned to keep you as one of their own."


## Hawaiians, no *Kānaka*, nah Hahh-Y-in

### for My Darling *Kūpuna*, the Beauties Aunty Bea and Aunty Kika

(manohman—da hahdest subject to write about in my liiife)
Iknow I goin get buss up fo diss because eeeEverybody like be *aliʻi*, I only like be *kolohe*. Dis jess my story, not da bessest, not the truest, jess mines.

Firs you gotta know my genealogy and dis buggah iss the hahdest.
I dunno my genealogy so much. I know I getdistant Mākoleokalani from *tūtū*, my
granma's sistah but to tell the truth, I jess not interested. Maybe because so late to know
and maybe I scared to find out.

Question: just WHO is Hah-why-an?
I saw a definition by Ronald (in his pitch letter for his calasssy publication) make the distinction of "colored"/"ethnic"—as oh sohard. He referred to his holiday "giving" letter
addressed to All Colored Authors whom he referred to as "diverse"—
What??? You cannoT understand what I try-ing to say?
—How you think I felt when I got the letta and my linguistic beagle mine was sniffing it out
and it jess sounded so fucken polite. iT Tried to be PC but it was silly.

So WHo iss Ha—Y—in?

Whoa man, I dunno.
As Kaʻai said, "You jess gotta be"                                    (so, vote!)
Sooner or lata, you goin find the one's trying too hard.
It takes no effort to be *Kanaka* (of course, arguable)
You born that way, like it or not: if I had *nānā*, paid attention to my pubic hair,
I would have felt more comfortable to be *kanaka* sooner.

Lastnight while I was gossiping with my cuz about Derrida and Hopkins—or ws it the other morning when we were discussing *"Mana* or Money?" that I told her about my conversation with the ancient poet K and our opinions about pubic hair. I said, "I should have paid more attention to my pubic hair than the hair on my head." which historically had been the "bob" or the "bun; the bun or the bob"—no other styles.

When Katie, the woman who cuts my hair suggested that I cut it the shape it is now in because

"It would make you look more dynamic."

I replied that I could not afford to be more dynamic:

"my husband would divorce me"—which he did.

But the point of this is that everytime I would cut my hair, the person who cut the hair always said,

"You have natural waves in your hair."

When I would go home to Hawai'i, the combination of salty, humidity, pollution, and my hair would make my hair what my older daughter refers to as "cotton candy hair."

So now that the hair on my head looks related to the hair in my crotch, I feel "together," "reassured," "belonging": now I have hair identity.

Or maybe, because I don't care about anything silly like my hair, *maybe* I am just being Hawaiian! or at least *kolohe*                    (please, vote)
I dunno.


When I was a young kid and was carried around the market in Chinatown, all the butchers would reach out their greasy hands with a chunk of *char siu* all the while adoring my eyebrows and sigh

*"Gahn liang."*

"Bee-u-to-ful, beautiful eyebrows," the old folks would echo.

**What?** did this all mean?


—that I was so ugly that I Had to have SOMETHING attractive about me; after all, the rest of my life, I was identified as being "stupid and ugly."—Like when you ask someone

"What does he look like?" and they translate

"Ugh-ly buggah" to "Shee has a wonderful personality."

When I check my eyebrows in the mirror, I can only wonder

"Is there ssSooo much *mana* in my eyebrows?"

The Hawaiians never mentioned anything about my eyebrows. Must be a Chinee thing.

People have been checking out my hair NOW because it is so weird. People say
"What's going on with 'the' hair?"
I say anything I want:
"It's making it's own decisions."
"It's *tres* Hawaiian."
"I'm going through my menopause."
"I'm in love." which could easily slip into "I'm gonna kill myself."
The lovely lady at Tom's Fortune Cookies where I always buy my chocolate
fortune cookies yesterday said to me (in Mandarin of course)
"You hair look good. You look ten years younger."
Nodding her own head in agreement with herself herSelf repeated.
"Look good," but I heard
"Look yaahhhyyaHHaaaghounnnng! hon-ney
Look hot! baby."
Without a thought I said,
"It's from eating all the chocolate fortune cookies."
And she smiling really did look beautiful: what she doesn't know is that
the more I visit her, the more Hawaiian she is becoming.

This section on **Hawaiian** is dedicated to Mike E. FunMahn (so
I can write off my legal fees) **because he always asking me "So
whatye doing for fun lately?"** (So here's the answer man.)

What then, Is Hawaiian?
Well, you have to know the postmodern Principle of *Pauhana* which is based
on the ancient proverb of ʻŌkole est ʻŌkole est ʻŌkole.                    (vote)

Lynn was so excited as he sat next to me at the Templebar when I searched for
my pen to scribble "The Principle of *Pauhana*" as a note to myself. The point
is that Hawaiians know how to *pauhana;* "in the *koko,*" the blood, as we say.
Unlike *Haole* and *Pākē,* and Japanee, when *hana* iss *pau, Kanaka* no like still
worry and work some moa. We like to clear the desktop as it were. Sooo many
times, it was *pauhana* time and the people around me were on Tokyo or New
York Stock Enchange time. Why? no need. On Sunday, Lynn and I was singing
and singing and laughing real loud. We burned our eyes staring at the ripe flesh
of the *hula* dancers who were doing bad-kine Las Vegas style *hula.* I said to Lynn
"Aye, dye wea-ing underwea-ah?"
Lynn said
"Either they have a G-string or have wrapped themselves at strategic points."

You should have seen it: the fat rolled up and over from all sides of the bra.
The *ʻōpū* wass talking: it said "You like feel?"
Throughout it all, the *poʻo* of Ka Nation was not amused. Such a pleasure not
be in the position of authority. I loved it and all the pleasure was based upon
my *ʻōkole* which was comfortable sagging in the bar stool. When it came time
to sing Don Ho's big hit "*E Lei Ka Lei Lei*," a very politically incorrect song, I
knew all the words and felt like I was still in the sixties when the song came
out. I got off the plane from my first year at college and when my girlfriend
arrived to pick me up, ALL the way home Carol Menezes' naturally flipped
hair was see-sawing back and forth, her body swaying while she was humming
"Ra-che-cha-cha-cha-cha-cha *e lei ka lei lei*."

Here is the secret of life (the part of the book where people have have to send $50. 00 to a secret
address to get the secret): if you have missed the Principle of Fun (on earth), then you have blown
the human experience. What then?
Go to hell.

### Ka mea Ka mea Ke mea Ka mea Ka mea Ka mea
### (this, why? that, how? whatever; when?)

Hawaiians living and breathing on today's planet now and then eat French
fries; have little interest in vertical formation and time management—no mo
dah verbs "to have" or
"to be" ass why.
We love to *lomi* a lot and kiss kiss kiss.
I love the Hawaiians. I love feeling Hawaiian—it's just so everything.

I love Hawaiians; sometimes, they burn me up. You know, it's that sacra-mon(e)y
of tourism *haole* kine ways that screws up the *naʻau*—what I translate to mean,
vision.

On the other hand, I just practicing English, man.
Why should Hawaiians be burdened with being the perfect Paradisian? Whenever I speak to my friend Lokelani, I start out by asking the first question on
every tourist's mind.
"How is paradise?"
Sometimes we evaluate "paradise" *en francais avec a peu d'ōlelo o Hawaiʻi. De
temps en temps nous parlons en anglais avec beaucoup de francais academie.*

Why should I write only about the Aloha parade stuff.

The Chinese were furious when I wrote about their evil small sides that you don't see up front when you go to the Chinese restaurant and eat that dee-licious food that makes you feel like you entered the Middle Kingdom above the earth and below heaven. Not being biased I don't feel any more sanctimonious about the Hawaiians although I do have a bit more *aloha* for us *kānaka*. (vote, 1996)

We going out in style. Maybe we will cry more than we can imagine because sometimes we just like a good one—man *we can* cry with that *hupēkole* nose runn-ning and not ashamed.

You should see Aunty Nani cry. Lyrical. Adiago. Ballet. *Kupuna* can drop crumbs on the tablecloth as she nibbles her bread and cioppino And with her pinkie—class act, man

                *haole* bettah watch and listen to this—

Aunty with her pinkie pick up those bread crumbs that look like gentle rain showers,

the flower shower trees of gentle

Hawaiian is always making love (not only Just the sexual kind but the)

*hā* and more hah, muscular, the physical heart like a transubstantiation of the bread and

wine and Mark got it too . . . in Kamau'u's writing rrright in Blossom's eyes

Just when you don't expect, it pops up in John Ogao

who is Puerto Rician Filipino and

There in Hanale's yummy body found in Morgan's wise and sweet tongue.

Davianna doesn't show it right away because her *mana* too powerful but little by little she will share her *mana'o* and her sweet voice.

It is in Uncle Walter's smile—his silence and him always blessing the food—how many times we sat in the restaurant and prayed!        VOTE

If you was Hawaiian, you would cry-smiling or maybe you need to hear it in my voice . . .

To be Hawaiian is to be very emotional because we love it.

Oh boy, Hawaiian is the greatest. *Nō ka 'oi!* The best.

Why you think the *haole* and Japanese like own our land? Why do you think they like have sex, marry us, and get da land easy way?

**Kūkā kūkā kūkā kūkā:**

Of course, no one prepared anyone to be disciplined by our *'aumākua*.

How did we know? *Nānā*, pay attention all the time.

No one gave us permission—to ask questions? *'A'ole.*
No one told the United States government to cut off da kine jets from our uncles and beat
up the ladies that like talk our sweet *ono 'ōlelo.*
Me, I'm one bloodhound: I like act out my frustration
*kūpale,* defend
correct, *pololei*
maybe appear to behave like an *'ōkole* until I find out Why and How things work: *hula*

I asked *kumu* (Naomi Kalama) about our *aloha.*
I confessed that it was so hard to be "natural" and to *mālama* everybody/every-thing. Too many people don't know that it is so natural for us to be nice.
*Kōkua:* to be present and helpful
*Pono:* to be in balanced with the gods and the natural world
*Lōkahi:* to be in harmony
*Laulima:* many hands working together

"Nice" is never enough for the non-*Kanaka* because
"the Other" always want "more" and not even Just More, because we are so good at giving
and hospitality and and and, MoRE is stretched to impossible dimensions and then
*'aumakua* and only then *'aumakua* must show a sign of *'a'ole.*

I hate this analytical part of me. Too bad I not one scientist, yah?
*Ono*-mouth Hawaiian as I am, I just went with my nose that led me to the good *wale wale,* the nutrients.

"*Hasa manana, hemo* de pajama."
Diversion. Diffusion. Nah, nah. Joke, joke.

## Laka, deity of the *hula*
*E kala mai ia'u,* forgive my crass interpretation of your art.
This is my *hula,* my *cyberhula,* my virtual reality *hula,*
my wrong *hula* that draws attention to
the *pilikia hula* that so many lost souls are leading and more lost souls are following.

*Ono Ono Girl's Hula* is danced on the keyboard in front of the monitor.
My *kumu* is my sister Lokelani *haumana,* student of *kumu hula* 'Iolani Luahine.

Our *'ōlelo* is horizontal and vertical simultaneously so as the in-house *waha nui,*
I render the full, true, and slightly crazy offering of the story.

The 1996 registration form for the Native Hawaiian vote reads
*Ho 'okūkulu he aupuni hou*
*Nāu nō e koho    i mua*
To build a new nation, The choice is yours


## Nelia and the Rat

**(Nelia, I hope you mean it when you say you love me. Here goes.)**

I mentioned Nelia before. She is the eldest cousin. Before she entered her pre-senior years, it was probably okay to describe her as my "oldest cousin." Now, it might be a bit touchy. But, she and her sister Beatrice are an unbeatable combination of laughs and tender bighearts. In their heyday, Nell travelled and always brought back exotic and always particular-for-me gifts: male and female Mexican and Indian dolls, which I passed on to my girls and are still alive on the shelf; castanets and those adorable-looking eensy, foul-tasting marzipan fruits! And while she was "on the mainland," "in Mongolia," "on a cruise in the Mediterranean," snapping slides of around the world, Beatrice calmed and fascinated me with Mozart, Tchaikovsky, Brahms, and other European nuts through her voice. The mixture of humidity and classical piano notes was enough to put me in a trance: regal, pretentious, Cinderella, and above all, smoothe soothe. What does piano music have to do with "Nelia and the rat"? Well, I can hardly imagine Nelia without Beatrice a heartbeat away. And she was more than a heartbeat that night. Beatrice was probably snoozing next to Dick in Kailua—or do they live in Kaneohe? What's the difference to an existentialist?

It was the middle of the night or maybe even approaching morning. Nelia, now in her sixties maybe. Slightly and gently (I'm so trying to tell the story and not outrage Nell and Bea, both literati), gently and slightly over a few on the scale, problems in the old legs, Nell has to use the bathroom. I do it all the time in the middle of the night. Nell has to go and when she turns on the light discovers

not a prowler in the conventional sense of the word but a guest. There, in her immaculate bathroom! There, a rapist!
There, creature from Hell, another test of will!
A (as my mother mentioned on the phone)
"a biiiiihhhhG rrrrRat. not a mouse, but a biiiiihhhhhGg Rat."

Where was Beatie?
Where were the brothers? Nelia, conqueror of the world. Adventurer on the Mekong
Delta. Nelia having gone up and down Huangshan in China under the worst possible conditions, Nelia Proceeded.
"Weeeeaakkk ssquuuuuaakk wheeeeekk," said the rat.
"Oh yeah"
challenged Nell in her nightgown hobbling.
"Weeeekk ssseeeaaakk," pleaded the rat.
Nelia having dealt daily with her own elderly mother now in her nineties; bathing, feeding,
loving: the works—this rat was peanuts.
"Life or death, nothing. This was a nuisance."
The story is that Nelia turned on the boiling water while the rat leaped from the toilet into the bathtub. From there, it was a cinch. Between the mop handle and three tubs of boiling hot water, the rat was massacred by my delicate-hearted cousin. The next day she called the Health Department whose personnel could only smirk and suggest pouring bleach down the toilet each evening before closing the lid. Humph, no respect.
Her nieces said that if that ever happened to them they would call 911.

Then my mother told me about Joe Mua (aka Moore) who has a tv or radio show in Hawai'i had disclosed that every time that there's a rat on an airplane, they have to catch the rat before the plane departs because no one wants the darn rat chewing any wiring to electrocute its dumb self while sending innocent locals into the volcano, the Ko'olau range, or god forbid, drowning in the ocean. If the plane made an emergency landing in Las Vegas, however, the rat would be forgiven.

When I told Nelia that I was writing pieces on Hawai'i and Hawaiians, that opened up the slop can.
Nell expressed both the irony and fear of thousands:
she said,

"Those Hawaiians are going to take our land away from us!"

Oh boy, it was not the time to begin calming her fears.
Instead, I reassured her that they would still need someone to kill rats and, shocked by my suggestion, we all laughed.

And that was what happened on Valentine's Day, 1993. Also, my husband gave me a cleaver and I gave him a quarter to ward off bad luck; and I gave him gold underwear which I almost sent to his office.
My mother and Nell and Bea got cymbidium orchids.
Eirelan, the spoiled brat, did not send me a thing. Ana wasn't much better, and my swollen heart sooner or later was spread in laughter forgetting any bitter flavor in the air.

## It All Depends What You Want

Eirelan said, "Mom, you require a lot"

# What! did that mean?
maybe, it *depends*    on what you expect
can tolerate and how long you can wait for what you want.
Abstract nerdism.

**To** be *multicultural,* or    **not** be?
I can *say* multicultural but what does that mean/and
what does multi-ethnic mean?
For those who do not speak two or more non-Euro languages, HOW and what can multicultural possibly mean?

Ma pa dofu (Chinese food), *duende* (a neat and spooky Spanish concept),
Luther    Vandross naked on the radio?

When Blacks start jiving, my ear has a talent for applause. I want to join the circus to indicate that I can *Creole* just as good *because.*
When I was a kid, my aunt would speak Hakka to me. But since I was not allowed to answer, I got accustomed to listening and after a while, I began to lose my tongue. Now, I can barely understand, can only hope to hop through a

few sounds to guess the message which is always a scissors at-the-heart-sort-of comment. And the laugh too. Now, I only measure. Now I only listen and try to fit the puzzle of any one language into the shape of another! Multiculturalism.

If you want to know a culture
learn the language
work in that country
stand in the long lines and be adjust to the greater reality
and maybe marry someone from the culture;
otherwise, the outcome is always narcissistic. You'll always judge the outside culture from your own native standards.

Metaphors change from language to language: conflict. Nature doing its *thang*. No one dares admit anything because it's more comfortable to pretend. So, factor in conflicts without solutions. Otherwise you're believing you got the real *thang*, but what you really got was computer-generated tv travelogue. The media wins again.

Don't we ever want to know the truth?

My friend in the red brick house warned me years ago.
She said, "Who wants to change. No one wants change."
And she and her lawyer husband happily go to France or England or now Italy.

Me? I don't even have a job. So much for wisdom.


## Dreams

Man, I've been having 'em. This recent batch originated its brewing in San Antonio when I dreamed that Hawaiians were supposed to come to a meeting and I knew that Tina would be there and (of course) she knew I would be there and son of a gun, she walked in with her *muʻumuʻu* (of course) with blond hair! And not only was it blond, it was blond and white at that. Beautiful.

In the next dream I was loving through leaves.
"*loving through leaves*" ass Right.

Leaves in the air.
Like I knew these were leaves on branches because—you ever ate seedless grapes or fish without bones? It was like leaves without branches.
Deep and cool greenish dark.
More like fans instead of leaves connected to invisible branches.
Like peacock feathers, but leaves. For sure. And, if I want to make more of it than I feel comfortable, I know that it was something to do with my 'aumakua allowing me to be more owl.
I'm more ready to be owl in my mouth and breasts.
And, I know that to be this way, I'm going to feel like that guy in "The Fly." You don't get to be something supernatural without losing some human feelings. And you can't have the easy parts either. The word, again, is marginalized. But I prefer freak.
I don't mind.


I'm gonna *kanikapila* with the *uku* in the *ukulele*.
I'm starting to feel closer to my *tūtū*.
When, the telephone rings and I say "Ah-loh-hah" People are so happy or they hang up.
Good. If people can't handle *aloha*, too bad. Imagine if I said *"Auhea aloha e"*—"Listen, I love you!" I thought Hawaiians were hundred per cent plus in intensity, but Grant said, "tousand per cent." Some Japanese good from Hawai'i. Uncle Peter, da best. I heard Mona iss preety good too. My mother's friend, Fay so so nice. Of coss, everybahdy know I love Milton. And Karen and Karen and Arlene, Ruby, Kara, and Cindy are the bestest Best secretaries at the UH Mānoa. Ov coss, Cindy is Filipina. Not all Buddhaheads or *pākē* or Potagese: bad. Some got good *pu'uwai*. The country ones stay good.


FLASH! Oh, my god.
I went home and my cousin told me that Tūtū's last name was Machado and I almost choked in the back seat of the car!
I knew there would be vowels in the lastname. I assumed there might be even quite a few but "Machado" was not what I had feared.
"Machado? Is like *malasadas*? My god! did I need to change my resume?"
And then when I came back here to upscaleland and was yakking with Victor who said, "If they told you you was Portuguese, you are probably Puerto Rican—lotta Puerto Ricans passing for Portuguese then." Aiyaa!

Months later, as I stare at the statue of my cousin Kalanihiapo infront of Liberty House at the Fort Street Mall, I am reassured to read "Mākolekalani"— *Hemeni*.

## *And den, I had dis odder dream* (Get Out Your Hankie) or for Bryan Joa-Chim

My husband and I
were living in a compound or apartment house that was structured like architecture from Hansel and Gretel with turrets, winding passages, secret doors, and backdoor stairs.
*Somehow,* we found ourselves
outside
in the rain in a effort to help someone.
Attempting to return into our apartment, we could neither find the way nor the apartment. I bumped into high-tech quarters that appeared to be built after the Marlon Brando Tahitian waterbed-by-the-sea. There were college-age white kids cavorting. There were jesters in costume but I could not find the space that my husband and I shared.
I tried and tried.
He and I bumped into each other struggling to locate it. I knew that he was becoming impatient and soon he was out of the dream.
The difference between the dream and reality is that I know soon he will be like yesterday's weather, but I do have some *ho'oponopono* to look forward to. Which is related to my lastnight's dream

This dream was full of adolecent boys and I was aware that they fully understood what I meant about "Dick, Jane, Mom, and Dad" being systemic in our behaviors and one by one: grandma, ma, me, my kids (not that abstract term "generationally")—the text we first learn to read—disembodies us.
Dick, Jane, mom, and dad have sex and their grandchildren
imbed in my English-speaking mouth.

In real life like the dream, the colored robots refuse to acknowledge I might be mentioning *something* worthwhile, if not valuable.

The white imprinted penises need to be cozy. Require cradling.

The multi-nah-shion-al-cult-eth Ken's and Barbi's not going to release any territorial gains.

Freud was WRONG (wots nu?). I do not have penis envy. I have penis waiver, breast liberation white man's kids and some kind of fun.

Even though I speak and write in English, I am always be teasing, testing, fooling around with English. I was a Slave of Love to Chinese. *Enfant terrible* as I am, I will probably challenge some aspects of my daling and mystical Hawaiian *ho'oponopono* or not.
Ain't that what artists do?

*I ka 'ōlelo no ke ola, i ka 'ōlelo no ka make*
"In the tongue life or death or danger or fun or vision or nothing or Something"


## WOMEN'S CYCLE TEA or she's gonna get her Period

Something happened to me in the fog when I wass wearing thermal wear and sitting in front the computer writing. I made a pot of tea and put it into the basket my friend gave us for our wedding. All day I drank that tea. I couldn't believe how happy I
was. It was not lightning zap or no one called or wrote to invite me to have a job but I was remarkably still, wrote and re-wrote, and was very content. I surprised myself. Though, not really. I have been praying to my *'aumākua* almost every day. I don't do it every day because I don't want to get into that ridged discipline followed by guilt habit that I have been trained in and flourish quite well.
In the morning usually and sometimes later in the day (Hakka *hua*, in Hakka dialect *shao heung*) I burn sticks with incense and visit all my relatives. First thing I ask for is to protect my poor house with the roof that needs to be recycled three years ago but so far, no mo money to do it. Then I ask for the job that is right for me.
I used to just say, "Please help me find a job."
And while I was praying, I realized that I need to ask for what I truly wanted. When Eirelan was graduating from college and had no idea what she was going to do except that last year I had casually positioned two books on boomerang kids in her bedroom—she was the one I was praying for the job. Now, she's in

Vermont. Big Shot for GAP, lives above a Caribbean restaurant, misses us and I goine bragg.

I always ask my ʻaumākua to protect the Terminator, Mildred. I named her that when I realized that nothing can smash her. She is still driving at eighty-nine and increasing her English. The other night on the telephone, she told me that she had a "phobia" about something. The last word she laid on me was not being able to "access" certain funds. Chinese always imperialize their relatives, brag about them as if they were gods. I suspect that they have missed out on I love you's and substitute godly words for real hugs and kisses. Mildred still cannot understand me but I believe she does love me.

*I am truly like no one I know*

I used to work it—remember that line from the "Fantasticks"—where the girl says "Please God, please, don't make me normal"?

For whatever reasons, my sister and I were not so close when she was alive. But we are now. I miss her a lot. I wish I could call her on the phone and hear her voice. So, I put gardenias by her picture and sometimes I place fruit or Hershey almond kisses on my chickenplate from childhood right by her.

And daddy's picture is in on my mirror in the bedroom. He has seen me and Steve do it everytime. Do I like that, maybe? My daddy had problems but when I learn about all the other childhood abuse and money problems of other folks, I know he did his job. And when I learned about the criminal treatment to Hawaiians, I know Daddy just kept it in. Poor, Daddy, sweet Daddy.
Aloha Daddy.

And I miss my Chinese Grandma so pretty. She really let me raise hell. And I miss my tūtū whom I never met. I miss my Tai Yi now and my dear dear Aunty Connie.

I was so scared of Big Uncle because he was so so Tall and what a tunnel of a voice! He demonstrated the sound of a pig's squeal just before death to tease me by the way he cranked his lungs in and out so I always ran inside my clothes. Aunty Dorothy was too smart and ma's family had no money. Perfectionist. Rule-keeper. Sometimes, she let a ray of sun open up and stun you. What a lot of Hakka!

I miss you Jacqueline
it's so lonely to be without you
I bet we could be laughing and loving so much

## Two *Hā'ole*: one on television; the other on radio

Lastnight when I was trying to fall asleep and who comes on the Bill Moyers show but Uncle Joe (Campbell). Ever since he started hanging out with the Grateful Dead, I thought someting was wrong with uncle so I lost interest in his *'ōlelo*. Lastnight but I musta been tired or *'aumakua* gave me something but lassnight Uncle Joe sounded better. Not like Uncle Carl (Jung), but approaching. Anywayz, I was really getting into my New Guinea sistas and brahhs and then, I fell asleep.

When I'm driving home from work today, Sista Jen/nifer was reading work on her radio show, KPFA, Dear, dear, *enfant terrible* KPFA. She gave me new acronyms such as FGM. The more she explained, the more intrigued I became. She enlightened me about the partial or complete female circumcision ritual in Africa and how it made some girls "less active." She ina-dition told about oppression and the guardians of oppression, in this case, grandmothers. Boy, was I glad that my family escaped from binding feet let alone Cutting the Clit which supposedly prevents sagging uterus!

Then, I was home and didn't want to write, re-write, or justify some intuition I had against any colored conservatism. So I turned on the tv and who was still on talking to Bill but Uncle Joe. He told a myth-ritual that included three days of chanting by villagers followed by the young men about to be initiated with one woman by having sex on an altar of sorts below some giant logs. After the last young man had sex with the woman, the logs were released so that the couple was crushed. It reminded me of the Aunty Nani story about the young Hawaiian lovers who made love and went into battle the next day. I also remember coming with my husband and crying hysterically and feeling so good at the same time. He thought I was delirious, but I knew, it was just culture. After Uncle Joe told the story, I was so scared he was going to tell another hot tip, I was forced to make love with my *'aumakua*. And that can show you what a nerd—shaman—I am.

Tell Carolyn a story. See what Carolyn does.

## Hawaiian *Piñata*

Ever since I could crawl and use my fingers to open things up, I have never stopped.

I always want to know secrets. Then, I can tell everyone else and make up my own secrets so no need to be so scared to know things.

When I was a kid on Coyne Street and punished most of the time, I had to have fun where I could find it. Frequently, it was in the yard full of odds and ends and sometimes it would be in the trash.

Every so often, I would see that *piñatas* were thrown away in the trash. Of course, I knew these were *piñatas*—the cheaper version—because I had seen them in the World Book Encyclopedia and also, Nelia had brought me one from her many trips abroad.

Every now and then, those *piñatas* appeared and Who and Why were they being thrown away?

Everybody knows there are gifts from faraway places in the layers surrounding each tightly wrapped candy or piece of magic paper that turns another color if placed in water.

Sometimes, there'd be the tinsiest cardboard doll or maybe a whistle. After several years of observing valuable treasure trounced into the stain and sourness of coffee grounds and chicken bones, I snatched the discarded *piñata* still tightly wound in its formidable shape.

How I remember the moment. The suspense was killing me.
No one was home except me and the *piñata*. My little fingers unrolled the black and white newspaper between me and mystery.

Oh, what was this! What a gift! What was this?
It looked like those things my mother kept under the bathroom sink.
Zwoonkk!
Hey, this was one of those things!
Hey, what's this bloody stuff on it?

Hey, this was one of those cotton headbands with blood,
stinky ssttinkkky old blood on it.

What kind of *piñata* was this!
While I was understanding what an unique *piñata* I beheld my older sister came
home and shrieked.
What on earth was I doing with her kotex?
Kotex? what was that!
She was going to tell Mommie on me for going through her private trash!
Private? trash? private trash?
How did I know who belonged to what!
This was my beloved *piñata* that I had rescued.
Talk about surprise!
Talk about let down down downer downest.
And worst part of it is when it was my time to have "private trash," I would
always
remember my first experience in the Error of Translation:
Period est non Piñata

# 2

# Parthenogenesis

## Practicing English

**How Will and How can I explain these sensations, these sounds that come out of my mouth that are** (as Victor says) "somewhere over the Pacific; they are not fully of here of this place called America. They are not fully of there either, of inner Beijing." **Where did my language come from?** By forty-eight, I realize that I was truly raised in a petri dish and my favorite conversations are like doing math. I can just break language down into phonemes, orthography, and cognitive processes (what else?), syntax, hermeneutics: and blame the 1941 version of **We Come and Go** featuring Mom, Dad, Dick, Jane, et al.

Authors Note: I have already written the introduction and have returned to insert this additional note because the longer I consider the issue and feel unsatisfied that I cannot best analyze and render my intentions regarding the development of my work, the more I can hear my Self tell me that I am creating new structures written in English that are raw and perhaps even threaten the good readers, writers and speakers of English (yes, 73 words in this sentence plus some). Furthermore, I have pity for those imitators of Good English who continue—out of ignorance, habit, or success—to first superimpose, then inbreed western faces of ethnicity, which creates new monsters of self-deception. I am absolutely certain about the risk I take when I write these words because an attentive reading and listening to the texts can all be tested and measured against *We Come and Go*. I am especially cautious to mention the listening part of the texts because if you "listen" to—at least the many Americanized Asian versions of—so-called ethnic writings, what you hear is an impersonation of, a habitual obedience of or a metallic rage against self-deceptive images. Who am I to say this? Perhaps, I leak this because the celebrated image of Asian America and Hawaiians (no such word in the Hawaiian language) has cut a swinging groove and somehow, for all our so-called wealth of resources, does not move forward. Our media image feels good.

**The history behind my hard to read writing:** according to my mother, I began talking at six months. Mother was relieved that I was talking—one- and two-syllable words in English and Chinese. Sooner or later, I was a tyrant. Eventually, only my Tai Yi, my mother's First Sister smuggled Hakka to me as she fed, bathed, and loved me because by pre-school, I was deep into elocution. Thus began my affair with language which has since gotten rid of friends, lovers, and two husbands who planned to possess me. Another part about me which deserves attention is that until 1987, the Hawaiian language was not official in my homeland. Why did daddy, *ō'olelo o Hawai'i*, speak Hawaiian, that low-class language outside the house? Why did he *sound* so spirited like he never sounded in English but never brought those ghosts inside the house? How come I never met any of my Hawaiian relatives except at Baby D's wedding—which I loved— and why was my sister so nuts to be dancing that crazy dance (the *hula*) when everyone knew it was stupid? So many unanswered questions.

By three or four, I was not permitted to speak Hakka, my mother's natural tongue: though my mother was a mathematician, she took speech classes at the University of Hawai'i just to make sure that she sounded "like a first-class citizen." What was that? What she never told me is that Hakka women are known as the "big feet, aggressive, and independent women" who were passed off as dangerous by the Cantonese. They are the only women who did not have their feet bound in China and currently can be seen under their black veils, the backbone of the construction industry in Hong Kong. So many women are still ashamed to be Hakka although they don't know why because their mothers couldn't or wouldn't tell them. And unlike me whom my husband calls the "Can Opener" (if there is a can of worms, Carolyn Lei-lanilau will open it without first asking permission), the others don't crave to know: they don't ask or forget why.

**But Tai Yi who whipped me with a *pīkake* bush stick after I broke the thermometer and was caught drinking what I believed to be cherry juice is the one who religiously seeded me with a desire for special-sounding, eating-like, vibrations in my body and swishable to feel from my inside**

**mouth floating, teasing, battling the outside forces.** She would make up words as she washed clothes with the wringer washingmachine. After bathing me (until I was about 10 or so) she would powder me and smell me, saying, "*So-nee mo-ko-li-li.*" It meant "I love your body," which she could not express in English nor did it exist as an expression in Hakka. She loved my life. She loved my smell and the food she fed me that grew into my round *moko* filled-with- life-body. *Moko* in Hawaiian means "filled with water," but Tai Yi made this feeling hers: she altered a Hawaiian word and made it local Chinese. The *so-nee* part is a half-word which is derived from the Hakka *hohn-sohn*, which means "sweat." It's always humid in Hawai'i and babies smell the best: a confusion of drool, snacks, the temperature of the day and the abundance of *moko* on the baby's body. What is the *li-li* part? It's Aunty's signature when she was letting her dragon-guard self down. It is Aunty's legacy for language invention. She who could barely spell her name but could read, lives on as her children, grandchildren, and great grandchildren chant her affectionate species describing this or that shouting or cooing her—phonemes and morphemes not knowing the construction or caring to know. **Tai Yi is in the blood.**

Now, for bi-lingualism. People who are naturally bi-lingual do not approach it as though the subject, verb, and object match. I mean, it is not Latin reproduced in every language, although scholars would have you believe this because this is their bread and butter. Hawaiian could never be reproduced in English because we do not have the verbs "to have" or "to be" in our language. Meditate on this as you're on the plane to "paradise." Back to the time when my Tai Yi beat me—do not confuse this word with "torture" or "abuse," I really do mean "spank" but she never hit me with her hands so I can't feel the "ank" sound of the hand against the fatty thigh. **I was more or less "whipped" and that never interfered with me from feeling any self-love but** early conflict did develop when Tai Yi whipping me would always remind me that I was "just like the Wilcox side of the family." In high school, I discovered my cousin Robert Wilcox led a rebellion against annexation and then I understood my link to my "dark side of the family." But to continue on the subject of bi-lingualism, after living in China with my French roommate Cathy and regularly mixing up French and Chinese; after being married to the contemporary prince of China and speaking international level English and Chinese with him while mixing cocktails of verbs and tenses—him imagining "schmooze" meant "smooth," I think my friend Victor said a lot about bi-lingualism, mutilated multiculturalism in "Snaps of Imagination," and there's a shot in Chen Kaige's movie "Yellow Earth" that tells me that **connections,** synapse, ssnaps are **the kick as the thumb and index finger** bounces jazz from the body. **Brief**. In fact, too brief. The song in the desert mountains, the contradiction of concrete and beach: too many vowels in the tight dress English. For me, it is the **wale wale**, the slime or nutrients in my *Kumulipo*, the Creation Prayers. **It is the sexual juices on, always on whether or not Mom or Dad can handle quite so many verbs without objects.**

Now that multiculturalisma is here, theoretically we have more than one concept sharing the bed and yard of Mom and Dad. **Now, we gonna have a lū'au**. No more English food. No more boiled meat in water with a carrot or potato. Non-sequential *salsa* in the cornflakes; *ku gua* on a picnic without punctuation; more bold *kolohe per sentence*; no more British comedy on public television. No more English sentences the way Mom and Dad would write them: no more English sentencing me to death. **The non-pure breads already are music and dancing and face and house and de and re constructivisms beyond our control on earth**. We are heaven. It be Blake and Aretha, rocks and owl policy. Nobody, no lizards, no money publishing house will be held to the left margin. **Maybe natural song will return in human voice.** *in the blood.* A new color on the page: same old 8 and a half by 11 but a more demanding syntax. Attentive in shape. Dunno. No standard yet. The real test is essay form, the serious convention. It is ass-sumed that poets are nuts—genius or space cadets—there has always been more interplay with text and form with poetry.

Get on your raincoat if you're scared. Don't go to the beaches; *the sharks are feeling safe to sing you love songs.* Gym-up for the *lū'au*, plenty of pelvic dancing and moaning. Where? in your body. But if you can only tolerate speaking and writing and hearing "good English"—it's like orgasm, gotta get messy to get it.

**Maybe my friend Sam Beckett said it in *Worstward Ho* somewhere near to what I'm trying to say:**

**As the soul once. The world once.**

This he wrote in yet another fragmented isolating and depressing piece. When I read "As the soul once. The world once." It was flowers and waterfalls and the rush of horses compared to whatelse he had been saying and continued to write. Being absolutely certain that you are connected to this life is brief, the moment both sustained and fleeting. Practicing English is as close as I can feel to this language in which I was raised, trained in, and formed a profession around. Maybe this isn't bad. Maybe it doesn't matter. Maybe it does but I won't be able to capture the form and symbols in English because maybe it is my body, the blood. Maybe it's like *hā*, the breath of life, Principle of Uncertainty, the feeling heaven, now.

Note: After teaching at the UH, speaking Hakka and Mandarin, Hawaiian and pidgin; cooking, washing, massaging, and learning obedience from Mildred this summer, I returned to Berkeley and on the first day go for take-out at King Yen. While I order the food in English—after some confusion—I correct the order in Mandarin. When the order arrives, the owner flirts with me in Chinese, saying, "The way you speak English is very good." Jet-lagged, shyly, I bend in the classic bowing of the head imagining my "Chinese" is very good—then freeze as the translation trails on the big screen—wha? huh?


## Everything There Is to Know about Love

There is not much to know about love.
There is everything to know how you behave with it each time. Some people I know would rather imagine a perfect life with a good job and money in the bank than experience any part of *it*. Others hopelessly wait for the best and keep heading for the buffet table expecting solid food, choosing dessert each time. Myself, I was doomed by the blue-eyed girls in the tampax ads as a kid. As the blond and blue-black-haired maidens cast their blue and white pupils towards a corner of the advertisement in the direction of white glossy stars in the blue-black-watercolored darkness, I felt a mad lush of surreal arrows pointing to LOVE!

The first time I was caught in love, I was captivated by the violet label of a 78 record playing, "Whenever we kiss . . ." and whatever the title *Moulin Rouge* meant, it didn't matter. At six, I was happily already in the leftover throes of *Malaguena*, "Beyond the Reef," and any possible mix of heartthrob magic. My poor head already suffering from the fumes of way too many flowers from above the mountain tops to beyond the shoreline. Green petals, warm greener hearts of *pakalana* percolating day and night within reach outside the window.
White ginger naturally deodorizing near the trash cans and Tahitian white, deep-throated yellow, rainbow, and pink plumeria underfoot
mix-breeding new fragrances with the humidity, new ideas and movements.
*Pakalōlō*—new excitements within old orders of good conduct.
I was wild as a baby and not any better as an adult.

The most fragrant Portuguese Chinese orange tree in the world grew next to my parents' bedroom. It bore a squeeze-your-face-into-a-knot sour fruit, but boy oh boy, you could eat the blossoms which tasted so sweet and the zing of the pistil inhaled coasted down your throat coated your insides like a shot of whiskey.

Whee ha!

Sometimes in the middle of the night, I would try to get my mother out of bed to come and sleep with me but as I approached to open the door, the crunch of the lock would startle me into realizing that the door was not about to open. Oh, oh: a royal jelly night!

While I never acquired proof that locked door, plus royal jelly found laying near the sandalwood box on the bureau the next day equaled something unparalleled in my winky-dink imagination, I have this *feeling* about oral sex that needs to be acted out that I will ask my mother when she comes in June for my younger daughter's graduation.

We will have our regulaire "Mon Diner Avec Andre" conversation to explore the universe again to see if we can still understand it all—new, old, and changing information.

## CAROLYN THE BAD ELDER

"The day after non-Thanksgiving," as the guy on KPFA described while playing one Indian tune after another—man I gotta say—those Indians are ssoo soo subtle because I couldn't really tell the variation of one drum style from another—I kept on waiting for the *ukulele* to break into tune after the Indians would wail "aye-yah, aye-yah"—I kept on anticipating for Aunty Harriet or Aunty Genoa to start in on that falsetto and taking off. No. It's different with the Indians: that much we don't have in common though we do have much. And then I played some *kahiko* and all I wanted to do was fuck though they are our sacred chants. So I cooled down with some Benedictines oohing and ahhing in Latin and I knew the meaning of those sounds "et unam sanctum" "Tantum Ergo." I could barely make out the meanings in the sounds of my own language but I could understand the prayers in the Roman language to the white guy with all that light around him, I mean "Him."

Today was another day though. I really want my husband to pay me some money—you know he "invested" at least lifetimes of my cash which my sweetie lawyer blinked his eyes and half-heartedly consoled me with "Carolyn, you're very trusting." Wasn't that sweet of him when in the second breath he sent me a bill in which out of a $2000 retainer, heh heh, I have—or had—a balance of $315! Gee, at least I can write about this huh! And at least there is the Emperor!

Well, I want some money because I have none left. So I beep John Good, the con man who now works at the Yellow Emperor Club. A few hours later he calls and I casually ask for any info about Steve and John Good says he doesn't know where Steve is. I ask if Steve is living with his girlfriend and John Good slurrs something like they split up a long time ago—"Oh so, now I can ask for an AIDS test huh?"—anything I can suck up from this scum of a human. No more info fo today. He no dumb Chinaman. I might have to invite him to dinner and put out a hundred-dollar bill to get more from him. I'll relax. Next in the plan, however, I use my all-purpose fail-proof weapon, the POSTCARD. It's time that I send Steve's parents, who owe me $500 and a few, a reminder to pay up, so I send his brother a message on a postcard which reads
"Dear Xu Wow, John Good, Steve's friend, warned me that your brother Xu Now has AIDS. No wonder he is hiding. So sorry for your whole family. Count on me as your friend."

I put on the little air mail sticker and saluted Admiral Nimitz. Who cares if he'll ever get it, everyone between will read it and the family will be ruined—at least I hope they'll be ruined. Or at least, it is my intention that some payback will happen from their thievery. Then I sang all the religious songs on the Elvis Christmas Album, "Peace in the Valley," "Take My Hand Precious Lord," and "It is No Secret (What God Can Do)." When Elvis was done, I sang all the Patsy Cline songs. Pretty soon, I will roll right into Aretha who will warm me up and tuck me in the Lord's everwelcoming embrace. Meanwhile, the postcard stayed on my desk: I wanted to hurt him Chinese style but if AIDS was the only way of hooking them, I felt ashamed of myself and just sent mean vibes.

See, it's not easy being an elder. Especially when you're called a baby all the time. The other day Mrs. Duck walked out of the bathroom at school holding her crotch and exclaimed, "WWow! Are you at student at Skyline High?"
I said, "Shut up."
Ever the clown she circled me wide-eyed and wouldn't stop. "Wow, you are so glamorous, so young."          "Shut—up," I countered.
But Mrs. Duck was rolling. "Why, it's too bad I'm not a man, I would run up to you and grab you."
"Oh yeah, Mrs. Duck, I'm gonna report you for sexual harassment!" I charged.

And we both walk away grinning smugly with our ability to speak English so well so quickly.

That Mrs. Duck, she must be Hakka. So so goddamn bold and funny and smart. Cantonese aren't as comfortable with themselves and the Northerners are so-so ji-ji-jittery.

I was actually going to write this essay about the beautiful and funny, smart and nice Ramona.
I told Ramona that I was going to introduce Myself as her
and while gasping she warned "Don't you dare!"
I tried it with Carol, one of Ramona's friends—who was NOT amused. So much for that effort. But I've always wanted to be Ramona since I first saw her and was instantly jealous. Smiling Tall, beautiful smiling hair and smile, and lately, muscles.
Beautiful sounding voice—all the time.
And when we were on the same funding committee: I was the barking dog; Ramona, the cooing dove.

Warm earth skin and usually neon-painted nails which go with the whole effect essentially. She's my big hope. If someone that good a catch is single—and my friend Connie too, if they are soo amazing and without being registered to one guy, that means something to me. Carolyn the Bad Elder doesn't think about these things so much, but every now and then especially when the white angels begin to fly invading My *Makahiki*—my rest period, my time for repose and meditation Hawaiian style; plus now, I'm sixty— that Hallmark Xmas begins to get slippery.
Anyways, I'm writing this for Ramona, the Goddess of Elders, Apricot Picker, Driver-in-the-night-to-San-Francisco-so-we-can-see "Lakota Woman."
Ramona Wilson, Colville.

Ramona, the funny, my dear dear friend—as all the suns and suns and moons and many moons have bowed and run away from us in our brief adventures together, may our ancestors keep us fed and happy.

May the ancestors provide more pleasure from your deep beauty—in the native meaning of this word.

May all living things help and praise you in your *salsa, samba*, and slip you from getting stuck on railroad tracks.

Until another project brings us together by land or sea—I send my blessings—
who Am I to send blessings?
Am I old enough to bless? What the heck, sister?

From one Native sister to another, across the ocean over the land,
My blessings and best powers to you forever.

Native Notes: since this was written, Ramona has met her Guy.


# An Official Indictment against the English Language
# Missionaries
# Sugar Plantation Owners
# the United States Government
# Development Investors and Tourists
# Who Are Sentenced to
# 'Ōlelo o Hawai'i and Hula
# through the Equipment of Contemporary Media
# with the Expectation
# to Perform the Traditions According to Kumu
# without Hint of Accent or Interpretation

# Before Swimming in or Sunbathing on the Blood
# of Hawaiian Waters and Hawaiian Land

in commemoration of
my beloved cousin Robert Kalanihiapo Wilcox

*Aloha!*

## *Almost* a Man

This essay is a response to the realization that I was born into Chinese, lived Hawaiian, and first learned to feel consciously and conceptually in French and use English (as in many cultures) only as a business tool. In every re-mapping there is a battlefield, and this space is mine: as a Native Hawaiian woman, I see that history proves that every treaty written by white men was meant to be broken. Therefore, every morpheme and phoneme on this white space is present as a stone or spear, rock, canoe, prayer, net, or spirit. Everything is meaning: limbs, an eye, fingernails, or teeth that *may* appear in the *western sense* of "excellence" and conquest, out of place. Translation: spelling, grammar, the presence or absence of diacritical marks and syntax in each particular language are <u>selectively altered</u>: I reproduce the convergences of many languages in my body, soul, desires on this or that subject. Read carefully. No be so proud and secure in thy accomplishments nor certain that the writer not in control of the format. Is thy thumb in thy mouth? Blame or influence from Blake, Beckett, Bukowski, Lu Xun, or pidgin which engaged me in a process that H. D. rallied, but for the exception of indirect behind the scenes non-policies—NGO's eh, women infact are rarely credited for any positive historic milestones. My aunts and mother have influenced my spiritual if not mathematic ways of approach, however. *Almost* A Man is because as a kid seduced by Latin my imagination catapulted me into ancient Rome through words like *civis*. Wow! a citizen when it (apparently) meant *something*. Oh the organic thrill to be creating and living language: you see this in artists, adolescents, and "in the community" all the time. I mean "network" and "on line" got no juice but when Black folks say "f-ool" with full oooph on the "f" and little or nothing sliding through the rest of the sound; and when folks from Hawai'i cut up, surf, jive English like they are peeping inside the underwear of English, tasting it and spitting it out: LANGUAGE be de power in the triumphs and wars; Caesar, the senators, and the conjugation of verbs. As *Bamboo Ridge's* (de temps en temps) avant-garde and bashful editors Darrell Lum and Eric Chock say again and again, it has to be good in the ears. Your body is eating and eating dat sound, dat more sound and rhythm. Itis the real stuff in poetry when your genitals and head feel *it*. O! O! I like one *now*. Primal man, primal.

Add to this the late-arriving realization that the globe (as I was taught as a child in accelerated classes) was civilized thanks to white men—mostly English, French, Spanish (the light-skinned, of course); Portuguese (however comical) enjoyed their share of conquest. Then there were sub-groups who thrive from conquest, which include (my favorite) the Chinese and Japanese, who are still ambitiously at work. These insights are what the "bookish Hawaiians" grapple with on an academic and personal level. Since I constantly write grants, I am capable of writing sequential sentences, but the larger question looms: would that ensure my own humanity? Having nearly completed the entirety of this essay, I realized that I forgot to include the most compelling strength of my writing, *'āina*, the land. If re-mapping is a true consideration of this issue of *Occident*, then a re-education and a return of Hawaiian land and sovereignty is necessary. As the genres of poetry, prose, and written and spoken word share the air and paper space more and more, I remembered that I could never separate *akua*, the gods/spirituality from *palapala*, paper. Therefore, I introduce my *mana'o*, my opinions with a statement in the body of a poem that manifests past and future in the moment of print where name or title supplies substance, though in English it appears as form; and in the Hawaiian language that does not contain the verbs "to have" nor "to be," the meaning of this introduction is when the Cazimeros sing "where forever means to stay, where forever starts today." As with the Romans, I conceived, I wrote and translated. *finis*.

### Ho'omākaukau REady

**Shihou wo zai gen wode 'ohana, je suis comfortable plus fort. Ecrivant cette statement, je commercerai:** Premierfois, francais et chinois ces les langues ecrier *rongyi* parce que ces langues sont tres scientifique, *you* medite *you* measurement. Ces langues sont langues de mon vie l'infant. J'ecoute et vivre dans chinoiserie et en retard, j'etudie en francais. En francais, mon coeur ecoute mon imagination. Eh bien, le mot pour "eggplant" c'est *aubergine*, le couleur de cet vegetable c'est ton nom. En chinois, le mot c'est *qie zi* mais, *qie zi shi* pour mon estomach pas pour mon yeux et mon *ear*. *Soyi aubergine zongshi yufa zai shucai*. Je comment regarde mon coeur. Si non pour mon coeur, *hui shenma bu?* Tous les monde ecrit les belles sentences. Pour quoi? Pas de lux. Pas de moment. Pas amour. Les petits soldats de morts ces dieux. Tous les choses dans les jolie places. Le govenor, madame et le president de l'universite sont heureux, les biblioteque marche commes mechanique et les etudients manage les baguettes jolie commes les fleures. Puis en puis, je vois moimeme une grandmere ou monsier de moyen age. C'es vrai. Repetez s'il you plait en anglais, en chinois. Etudiez les formes formidable.

Zai Meiguo wo bu yau *l'idee de* bai ma fei ma. Ma shi ma: fei shi fei; bai ma, hei ma, hong ma; ma shi ma. C'est mathematique. Bu Zai Zhong Guo, bai ma shi bai ma. Shi hou zai Zhong guo, wo you tan tan gen *mes amis tres vitale tres intime—j'oublie mes penses regarde le blanc cheval pas le blanc cheval.* Wo hen xiang "Ah Q." Shenma dungxi gei wo jei ge raison ecriver cet articletres non comprehenez? Encore fois, c'est mon coeur. wode xin. Pu'uwai.

Je reconnais ecrivez, ecoutez et parler la langue Hawaiian parce ce que mon coeur est dans cet mysterieuse. Images de la mer *(wai kai)*, les chansons *(mele)*, ma famille *('ohana)* da jia 'ohana, ma mere ma tres bonne mere, wo ma—c'est vrai a cause de finalement, wo nung ai wode shuofa, wo nung renshi les vents et les montaignes, les accents et les epeles des mots. Pas d'anglais. Anglais a rien pour moi. Cet an instrument d'argent. Hier matin, quand j'ecoute la radio, personne parle en anglais. *"What is the problem with being an American? Forget all the Afro-American, Japanese-American, Mexican-American stuff. My daddy taught me that we are American. If you go up to a counter at MacDonald's and want to order a hamburger and fries, you should be able to get a hamburger and fries without hearing any filipino being spoken."* Cela suffit. Je suis fin. Je savoir faire parler, *"I want a hamburger and fries."* C'est dommage, personne en radio station est oublie le premiere fois. Californie c'est un place Indian ou Mexican. Peut etre nous somes parlons epanades, pour quoi non?

Eh bien, you tai dou dungxi wo xiquan attend: la rue entre l'un dee et le coeur et les beaucoup des images*īgen\* hā a pu'uwai.* Maintenant je sais apes j'ecri mes desires et mes pensees vraiment en quatre langues, c'est entendu tres difficile vivre vraiment pas avec *conflict.* Chaque langues *you* chaque circumstance peut-etre pas exist en un autre langues. However, si vous vois le film *waiguoren et nian jei ge wen zi, wen zi bu shi shou fa,* rien. Pour le monde pas interesant ecriter, eudier, parler les abstracts, les ecrit mots pas de purpose souyi, il n'avez pas raison d'etre. Cette langue c'est une langue comme une langue belle de jour. Personne desire ecoute cette, danse les syllables et les rythms. Pour moi, mon premier langue jusqu'a mort yin wei c'etait celui comme langue. Tres intime, tres bonne, tres *bu ai gen waiguoren.* Maintenant, je suis veille, je sais faire beaucoup de chose.

### Traduisez

There is always some survey or study based on the poor girls who like math or science. How about pitying the female slaves of linguistics and philosophy: we are invisible because you have to be a man to be invited into this club. It's kind of like the Junior League of erudite snobbery. The qualifications are that you are insecure about each stroke or sound which may represent concept and you must be prepared to defend the impulses in your brain without confusing them with the impulses of your groin. How would I know this since I have no certification in rhetoric, philosophy, or *whatever*. Of course not, if anyone certified this woman, this Hawaiian/Hakka feminist to teach at a university, I would have men practicing the art of folding underwear during the first class. My *mana'o*, this essay, is entitled *"Almost a Man"* because, like a pilgrim or pioneer, it was through male-developed, male-dominated Latin, English, and Chinese that, believing in the written rules of each language, I searched for respite and found myself instead a sojourner. Currently, I am studying Hawaiian and some Maidu (Northern California Native American), and I have never been more fulfulled and happy day per day. I feel like *Almost* a Man because I have tried to be equal footing of men: malfunction. I have tried to serve men: they don't deserve it. You know the routine: if a man starts to burp around you, run. It is only moments before the farts and snoring begin to suffocate a woman's air space. I am sympathetic to all my dearest male friends—kind, bright, loving, doubtful about their steadfast qualities because in the eyes of other men, they appear to be *almost men*. Of course, we could still try to be like Romans but why, hauh? Let us citizens of language untie the mannacles of English syntax, name it guerilla consciousness or *fiesta* in the ears: we earthquake-proof the disintergrations of language or get used to being a robot.

### *Ecoutez*

When I was with my family in Hawai'i, I was very very comfortable. Just writing this statement brings comfort to me: first French and Chinese are easy languages because they are very scientific: millennia of thinking and measurement behind these suckers which were the veins and arteries of my childhood. I listened and performed in Chinese then I studied in French. Through French, my romantic heart heard my imagination. For example, the word for "eggplant"—an ugly word and sound in English is *aubergine*, also a color and feeling of the round vegetable. Therefore, this name feels as Goldilocks herself might have claimed "just right." In Chinese, this same chewy *comme* squashy vegetable is called $qie$ $zi$, which is the sound of the cooked vegetable swooshing its way into the mouth and the suck toward the throat. My Chinese husband proudly announced that no one was going to tell him how to eat or fuck, which is the origin of the reason why $qie$ $zi$ was so named.

## Get Chance?

Suck suck suck or is it?
fuck fuckfuck, yeah, yeh yh more fuck
more suck more squash.

After my husband last fucked me, he asked straightaway about our divorce. I reminded him that I had just enjoyed myorgasm and wasn't too operative. Then mymother called and I had to tell her that I had completed havingsex with my husband and she inquired, "Do you really have to have sex?" "Yes, i do." Ikindly replied

Then she started asking if I had taken care of the United Airlines' coupons and I had to inform her that I had just completed orgasm and was not fully functional. "*Poi!*" she replied "okay, okay, Now, I can go to bed."

When I told my husband the story, he said, "Carolyn, you have to learn to say 'I'll talk to you later.'" I said "No, my mother and I are extremely close. She always knows when something's up. If I don't tell her that I can't function and why I can't, she'll be worried that I'm witholding something and by the next day will remind me how she suffered by not knowing my state of health." So, it was more "energy efficient" to tell her that I had had an orgasm. This is what is known as "enjoying sovereignty" among linguists and smiling a little bit simultaneously. The Chinese are not so much an eye or ear people as a stomach and counting numbers type. And as my husband walked down the steps, he turned to me and cautioned

"I'm from barbarian. I'm trained like a circus animal, but I can turn around and eat you." Then he kissed and huggedme. Well, I *guess* that I had better remember that proclamation. Gee, the guy had just gotten in touch with my most erotic psyche, tapped the pulse and freed me from months of believing I am a paramecium. And jess like that, he rewinds the video of the Chinese opera between us whereby he must dominate and I must lead. Now you know why *aubergine* will always be in the realm of vegetables, never a topic of philosophy. Primal man, primal, said the *haole*.

## Ha 'ina Mai Ana Ka Puana,  Tell the Story

I need to mention something about my *na'au*, my instinctive heart: if it wasn't for my heart or maybe I might mean instinct, why exist? No matter how advanced computer robots become, they cannot create warmth from their own decisions. The genius of technolobby and educated humans is that "they" can execute functional sentences called legal documents. Why? Not for breath or moment. Not love. These gods (sentences) are midget soldiers bearing death.

These soldiers inhabit the pretty exterior: image. The boss, mr. and mrs. president of the university are smiling; libraries function like a machine and the ones who are the clothing of students eat pretty bread with flowers. Little by little, I see myself as a grandmother or mister of the middle ages. It's true. Repeat in English and Chinese. Study convention.

### A Little Something *for Literary Criticism*

In America, I didn't accept the idea that a white horse is not a horse. Horse equals horse. Fat is fat. White horse, black horse, red horse—a horse is a horse. It's logical. But not in China; a white horse is not, could never be, will never be a horse. In China, I had long engaging discussions with my colleagues regarding the subject. I can't remember what had convinced me that the white horse was *not* a horse. It was probably a matter of infatuation or survival against a tirade in English and Chinese during which I had to be converted to understand the position—after all, I was in China. A footnote impulse: around 1987 or 88, Shorty Deng—the one who ran the ditto machine during the Revolution (because he was the right size)—formally known as Deng Xiao Ping flipped-flopped this conundrum to read "It doesn't matter if a cat is black or white as long as it can catch mice." You know the guy, he's the same Communist that said, "To be rich is glorious." Who gives me more power to write? the Chinese? the Hawaiians? the Portuguese? I'm like Ah Q who conferred upon me the logic to write this essay difficult—maybe impossible to understand.

For the sake of literary history, I need to mention some critical data because no one has ever inquired about this factor in the criticism of my work (heh heh, like there's any because who can understand it, eh?). When I am written about ina collection of Asian American or Chinese American writers, I am lumped with vast land and mucosa of yellow-tinted dark-haired humans who at one time were generally influenced by Kung Fuzi, Confucius. A significant majority of these humans who immigrated to the continental United States as well as my homeland Hawai'i were Cantonese. A majority of the Chinese American writers are Cantonese. I am not Cantonese. I am Hakka and Uygur.

One especially interesting minority people are the Hakkas, who are widespread in the south and southeastern coastal areas. They are thought

to be twelfth-century migrants out of North China who insulated themselves from the surrounding population and clannishly preserved many
of the "pure" old style North China ways.

> *China's Imperial Past*, Charles O. Hucker

and if you don't know who Hucker is, you will definitely know John King
Fairbank whom I'll quote from his last book, *China: A New History:*

> . . . migrants from North China several centuries before, who retained a
> northern dialect and other ethnic traits, like opposition to footbinding.
> As a minority in South China, the scattered Hakka communities were
> uncommonly sturdy and enterprising, as well as experienced in defending
> themselves against their hostile neighbors.

Who were these "neighbors"? the Cantonese. And in Hawai'i, the Cantonese
treated the Hakka the same way the Japanese treat the Okinawans. I could
never say that I was Hakka. Never spoke Hakka in public. Was discouraged
from speaking Hakka and thank god beaten by my First Aunt with a *pīkake* stick
when I didn't speak Hakka. Thank god for those beatings because now when I
go home, I am the only one in my generation who can talk with the aunties in
their high eighties. After that, I have my cousins Nelia and Beatrice from whom
I suck every sound and gesture because the Hakka spoken in Hawai'i cannot
be duplicated: it has its own linguistic twitches and idioms; and influenced by
the Hawaiian language and pidgin, my family makes up words. I wrote an essay
on this subject in *Blue Mesa Review* no. 6 if you want to know the hermeneutic
implications.

I had to first study Chinese history then study Mandarin here in California to
discover these pieces because in Hawai'i we are so nice and so oppressed that
no one could tell me this because there was an understanding: don't be so *niele*,
to keep asking questions, or *maha'oi*, bold in questioning. In Hawai'i I couldn't
imagine or dare ask the question and there were no sociolinguistic leaks around
me that indicated an insight to the potential questions. So I had to come here to
learn that Hakka is not only okay but wonderful, as Fairbank further indicates:

> The most original corps of Hakka true believers were the bravest in battle
> and the most considerate toward the common people.

So that's my mother's side. My father's side is Hawaiian and Turk. The Uygurs
from Northwest China are not Han. How did someone from Northwest China

get to Hawai'i? Somebody's gotta be first I guess. They did it then and it's jess in the genes I guess. *A'ole*, no I am not your average Asian American nor Asian American writer.

I'm owl.

Again and again beats my heart.

My measured Chinese heart, my primal Hawaiian heart, the only heart I know.

Talk about heart, body, blood, and Hawaiian, I hope all you get a chance to meet the *kia 'āina* Mililani Trask. Never in my life did I ever expect to meet someone who represents me that I love and respect. She is so smart; a good listener and patient. If you see her in her lawyer persona in "Mililani look" perplexed (by all the outrageous stuffs her rational mind is intaking) and (processing all of the English into translated Hawaiian so that she will) not (be) perplexed because she knows we are the last generation. The *po'o* said, "Face it Carolyn, we are a dying race." Now those of you who have been to Hawai'i and maybe planning to go there, *nānā*—pay attention, I didn't write the title of my *aloha* poem for nothing. We are ending and the tourist industry and multi-nationals are winning. After us, we are not going to be dancing *hula* for you anymore. You can only play those Hawaiian Airlines and Ed Hogan tv commercials to remember how we *used* to dress up to bring you to Hawai'i. And those people rushing to Kaua'i with their damn crystals are wrecking that island. Aye, you like go vacation, go Bosnia. You like hot weather, go Palm Springs or Arizona. Go to Nevada like all the poor Hawaiians who can't afford to live in Hawai'i.

# Don't
don't     don't don't dnt dt     **come to Hawai'i.**
## DO:     NOT COME TO HAWAI'I and
complain about dis or dat. And please don't move to Hawai'i and buy our land when our own people cannot afford to live where we're born.

If you like to feel *informed*, read the Hawaiian historian Lilikalā Kame'eleihiwa's quintessential text, *Native Land and Foreign Desire: Pehea Lā E Pono Ai?* Pretty good, eh, statement in one language; question in another.

> At the same time that Dening builds Marquesan models, he also explores the structures that underlie the white man's reality and his metaphors. By presenting the two realities side by side, Dening creates a more plausible reconstruction of the historical events. He continually reminds us that in the Pacific there are at least two distinct realities from which any event can be viewed, and that the transfer of metaphor from one culture to another is rarely unaccompanied by some sort of violence.

**Writers beware**: no be *lōlō*. We get one list of all the writers who imagine they could get away with writing about *Papa* and *Wākea*, our Mother and Father stealing any of our *'ōlelo*, or concepts so you can sell your stupid *puke*. Our *'aumākua* watching. Just like you no take *pōhaku* from the Pele's body, the volcano, or swim where get undertows and undercurrents, **do not borrow, steal, staple, tape,** *imagine* **you can** with your fingers write our *mana* in y**our** **language and commodify it**. Remember, eh because someday Something going happen sometime so don't come running to me because I goin laugh and say, S'why hard: *ou cela pourquoi difficile:*
I told you.

### Ha'ina Mai Ana Ka Puana, Tell it, Geeve 'em

I remember writing, listening—dancing a Hawaiian language, a mystery. Images of water, the sea, the voices of my family—my entire family, my daddy finally happy and my sister whose *kumu* was 'Iolani Luahine, my mother wonderful! wonderful—it's true because finally I can love the way I organize my self-expressions. I sense wind and mountains, the accents and spelling of words. Sometimes I won't complete a sentence because I'm bringing the whole me into English which is dead—just look at the state of the English monarchy. And those Brits are nuts wearing those wigs and dresses and so uncertain about their sexuality. English is no fun—though I am beginning to like white men again (and if that certain young white boy who likes me gets a hair cut like the guy whom he looks like in the current *Details*—maybe he can score), having been tortured recently by male Koreans who insist that English accommodate their every impulse. And, while I like the image of Latin men in movies and television, my good-looking Chicano activist beau who rallies for legions of abstract masses in Chiapas—could Arnoldo ever show up as promised? It was the same with the famous Puerto Rican writer: it is impossible for a woman to be smart and sexual and be in an okay relationship with a guy. One or the other is okay, but the combination is toxic to the best examplar of guy. I know it is weighty to state that English suffocates me; however, when the vigor of Latin resurrects like a volcano and the action of the foot soldiers and agricola and war and the sea and every tone and variation of "amo" breaks loose in the delivery, English be bahd. Maybe that's why I like to hear English spoken with an accent because then there is some sound and rhythm in English. I even love to hear my friend Robert—the enemy from England And a relative of Captain

Cook—I love to hear him speak. I know exactly what to predict and when he startles me, I can say, "I hate Shakespear." Robert doesn't care. English and Englishmen are not important to him. I am important to him! He can read and write. When he rings me on the telly, his messages are impeccable. First, the pausing breath before the greeting "Good afternoon." Then the *C'est moi*, which in French translates to mean "It's me," as opposed to "C'est je" which means "It is I." Robert says, "It-is . . . I—and I have a white sweater which I have washed and has beautifully aired in the sun and needs to be returned, I am well. I am well and have kept away while my heavy cold was potent but I'm well. Hope to see you soon. Bye bye." Poor guy, I told him I couldn't see him if he was sick.

I also like my friend Julie—Hungarian from Australia who was educated at Dartington Hall, the Summerhill equivalent, and lives in her own cosmogony— who gave me advice about my husband: "Carolyn, if you want to have sex with him, there's the phone you know. I mean, what man will turn down sex? You say 'I want it' and he will be overjoyed to deliver. Especially when you indicate that what you want is an animal relationship with him and nothing romantic or meaningful—I can't imagine that he would refuse you."

Meanwhile judging from the likes of in-house literati, English is so bourgeois. Paper paper paper or books, journals, readings—that's all *l'autre* literati know. Come into the "community" and see if you can hang. When we are in the community—wherever it is—we are at home. Oh it is complex all right, but if you are an ad-min-is-trator, an academician, or just an ordinary pale face, maybe the "community" is like a foreign film. Or . . . maybe the perfect English speakers are so constipated because they read too much. I mean, what is the problem? Historians, psychologists, news anchors can use the word "white man" but get a white writer to pronounce that term—no can, no way. They don't consider themselves white: they see themselves as "liberal" or "progressive" and they don't want to identify themselves as "white." Maybe because then they have to admit that they get all the power, eh? The soft sell is that only "the best" were privy to Latin I and never approached Latin III where the orgies and debauchery really got fine-tuned. Eh, but look at the Latin scholars, not one Andy Garcia or Darrell Strawberry among the lot. I mean, Who names their kid Catullus, Horace, Seneca, or Tacitus? Years ago I walked across that Berkeley campus when I saw the homeliest humans. Why are intellectuals so ugly lookin? *Finis.*

Good English means good money. When I was listening to the radio, someone called in and said in English, "What is the problem with being an American?

Forget all the Afro-American, Japanese-American, Mexican-American stuff. My daddy taught me that we are American. If you go up to a counter at a MacDonald's and want to order a hamburger and fries, you should be able to get a hamburger and fries without hearing any filipino being spoken." Maybe the caller didn't realize that Sony now owns MacDonald's and it was the 'Mericans that sold it. In *Manifesto for Pidgin English*, Leialoha Apo Perkins really punctured English kine chains—the same manacles that William Blake fought against—

> Maybe English is communication too, but I no can see dat dat's w'at
> you make 'em. Iss like one stick fo' beat us so we work fo' you.

> Mistah Holmes, no teaching nobody heah English. You teaching *haole*.

Kaleo knew tht he was going to be late for the hui meeting. But that was because he didn't care. From what he had learned that morning,

# a man has to be a man no matter what his language

Oh English, English, English, I have conquered your ridges and heights because I am able to say "I want a hamburger and fries." Too bad radio host forgot the first memory, most important: California is first Native American—always will be Indian. Maybe I should have written this in Spanish—or Ohlone as in the dialect of this area instead of this bad breath English.

**Hana hou Aa-gain!** There is another matter that I'd like to address: the area between the idea and heart and the many images with the breath of life and heart—for now, I'm able to write my desires and my true thoughts in four languages. Of course it's insane to live this life of cultural tangle, extraordinary sex brittled with *soignée* from time to time. The payoff is seeing how heated people get defending their own speech. ha'h! Each language has each circumstance that perhaps does not exist in another language. But what does integration mean after all? Living with difference. Don't the French hail "Vivre la difference!"

If you watching a foreign film and read the sub-titles, the subs do not exactly reflect what the actors are saying.

The days of Momdaddickand janeSallyspotand puff are *pau*: Mom is a lesbian. Dad is schizophrenic. Dick is an alcoholic and get this—cannot read. What's the future of the nation? Jane is a ho. Sally driving da Volvo administrator for an ethnic 501 (c) 3—she filed chapter 11. English got no purpose in function no mo. No mo ozone, no mo rainforest. Puff and Spot designer food "out" them in therapy; and less money, less opportunity, less respect from *l'autre* mean mo for us. "Less is more," now that's a saying that we the insects make art from. Pidgin, not esperanto, not Latin or English or Mandarin or Japanese or German gonna be de language of Life—my body's grew up on dat slackened key in my voice and body oiling all parts of me. I'm from the *wale wale*, the sexual nutrients—that raw *ono*, good eating, and also Hakka, "Those big feet, aggressive, and fiercely independent women." Not too late for you to imitate me and have a little fun, *akamai*, but

*"I ka 'ōlelo no ke ola, i ka 'ōlelo no ka make."*
"In the word, life or death"
**Pau hana**
**i mua!**

<br>

$$
\begin{array}{c}
a \\
m \\
a \\
l \\
\bar{a} \\
M \qquad\qquad\qquad\qquad \text{'āina}
\end{array}
$$

M
ā
l
a
m a pono

<br><br>

**a hui hou**

—this was originally

dedicated to my cousin Robert Kalanihiapo Wilcox, who fought for Queen Lili'uokalani against annexation in 1889. Now I add Zhang Ziqing, Professor of American Poetry at Nanjing University in China, and my daughter Kalea-Qyana Manning.

# 3

## Practicing English

### What? *Shenma?* not even *Hui Shenma?* WhY

I'll divide my lives in China into three categories, as Chinese are fond of both measurement and sequence. (Man) Chinese always reconstruct a story with the pretext of understanding framework and timeline while acquiring ammo to criticize or lecture if they get impatient with the story.

In 1983—it may as well have been 1893 or 893, mother suggested that I go on a long trip to heal my heart from my divorce—the first divorce in my mother's family. What a better place (for the length, education, tour of all the provinces, and especially the price, considering the exchange rate) than the Middle Kingdom. In 1983, when I went to JU (Jinan University), China was just as much of a dump as it is today, but it was charming. It was completely unpredictable as it is today, but there was a simplicity and honesty that made me both proud that I was Chinese and embarrassed that I could not speak one of the dialects. As an American, I was encouraged to achieve and succeed in English not in Chinese. Moreover, having grown up in Hawai'i, my parents were determined that I flourish without any stigma, so, like many other Chinese of my generation, I knew what Chinese foods were good to eat but I could not speak Chinese. Adding to this, the Chinese schools in Hawai'i taught Cantonese and my mother spoke Hakka. Punti was a dialect of Cantonese, and the Punti and Hakka were rivals. You only heard bad things about the Hakka in those days—actually some of my cousins still suffer from Hakka inferiority complex. I wanted to—and can still—speak a little Hakka, which is essentially a dying language. Having migrated from the north in the twelfth century, when they arrived in the south they refused to assimilate with the Punti. In addition, Hakka women were the only sensible ones who refused to bind their feet and eventually were identified as "big feet, fierce, aggressive, and independent." My feet are small, but I think those characteristics run deep in the genes because my mother always reminds me of the proverb that grandma told my own mother: "Just because you cut grass and shove it in someone's mouth, you don't have to tell them what they're eating." So, after uttering even less than the common "Ai ya" on the first trip and surrendering to the poetic in the former T'ang digs, I returned to Amelika to plunge into Chinese language, history, lit, philosophy, and men.

But more of the first time first. WEll, I never went to the orientation meeting and Prof. Zhang accused me of being rebellious. No, I had no intention of being rebellious, I just missed the meeting and wasn't aware that it happened. Besides, my boyfriend was requiring a lot of me at the time. As a gift, he cut some of his pubic hair and stuffed it into a tiny red envelope. When I was lonely or frustrated or just devious, I would open up the red package and talk to his brown wavy pubic hair. Years later, I forgot about the hair and sent the same red package with fifty dollars in it to my mother as a gift. You can imagine (and probably smirk that I deserved) the horror of my mother telephoning and asking what the meaning of the hair was! Of course, I could only gulp and assure her that it was my daughter's hair from the time when she was a child! Yikes, caught or at least nearly caught again. Nonetheless, at this orientation meeting, I guess we were advised on what and what not to expect. What did I know when I got to the airport?

After the long ride with too many meals, we land in Hong Kong followed by the choo-choo ride into the Big Country. What an intro! those first few moments on the soft seats with lace and delicious food under formal 1920 British comforts inside with stunning miles of rice paddies, water buffalos, stretches of dirt road lined with militant poplars. It was summer—I always seem to be there in the summer—and my body and imagination were exploding. The timeless country sky and slow pace that urban humans supposedly crave, a meditative quiet so profound—I was in a famous/common brushpainting, a poet in the landscape:

everything I could possibly want in *my* dream. It was *my* dream because most of the other Chinese Mericans did not like this place. That was in 1983, the first time; the sweetest love, the beauty still young.

Of course, I can ramble city by city (I may as well become a historian) but choose to highlight the cities by realm of symbols as opposed to what was bought or seen. These then were some of the symbols: me in the triangular scarf as a halter top; my bathing suit top interpreted as bra; pissing in the middle of the night with a 100-plus fever in Mongolia and riding the horses the next day. In Mongolia, too, the mosque shapes at the railroad station in the call of *allah*; the endless giant sky defining the green waving grasses sprinkled with cotton puffs of sheep. In Hangzhou and on the Great Wall, I flew kites; and discovered my skills as a photographer in Jingdezhen, later showing up at a meeting wearing a bedsheet because our luggage had not arrived. Also in Jingdezhen, the perfect house constructed entirely of fitted wood and beautiful rows of unpainted porcelain drying in the shed, mauve shadows in each sharing the battle of wood and clay. Probably the real highlights cannot be mentioned, but there were many ancient gongs echoing, like the gentleman at the Summer Palace minding his own business who sat cross-legged in that real Chinese style, feet propped on a stone pillow (as opposed to the perpendicular Americanized ankle at the knee). His clothes were willowy—long short-sleeved white shirt, the correct washed-out grey pants, white socks, and opera style black cotton day shoes. A wide-brim straw hat kept the sun from his face and he rested on a deep green park bench under a cassia tree. God, he was elegant. Nothing common about that treasure. Even the sun rested on the right branches to cast favor in his direction. Luckily no one noticed until I took his picture, then all the busloads of tourists intruded upon his privacy—which is impossible to come by in China and I ruined it for him. Of course, I was ashamed. I was greedy. So what if I had a talented eye: I was young and selfish. It was my first trip. A close friend who's an anthropologist informed me that there are three levels of knowing a culture: first, by staying in public places and riding public transportation; next, by being a worker; and finally, by marrying into the culture.

That was the romantic part. Huangshan, climbing Yellow Mountain was the challenge. First off, I experienced "error in translation" during this "nature hike" where Thousands of tourists—mostly Asians—herd side by side, up and down many very steep mountain paths, often only two feet wide; and then you get to fall off the mountain if you get distracted, shoved (common), or pause to philosophize. Every step I took I wondered, "How the hell did I get into this?"

With my porter carrying my backpack, almost down to no water except to stare bewildered at the urine cocktails floating down the occasional streams; hot and humid, that is hot hot and humid; giant marigold, damsel midnight, race-car red—butterflies the size of your hand would sweep across your eyes and it was like being *National Geographic!* There I was, short, deliriously absorbing culture and history; the ping pong of sweet and choppy Japanese mummering in among the loud and gruff Mandarin; whining and bargaining Cantonese; bird solos and of course, the stares. It was so Chaucer but in translation. People were spitting and farting. If there was an earthquake, we were doomed. Sometimes, you'd see porters carrying up whole sides of decks to be assembled at the stopping points where there were hotels—fifth rate, but ready to serve the masses who made it to the top for the night, who would then fight and race to the lookout points and snap shots at sundown while I sat behind planning to walk down by myself the next day. It's not so much that I like being alone, but I cannot behave well if I feel too compressed by crowds.

Now that it's safe to say, I was a real American artist during that first trip. I qualify myself because unlike the other Chinese Amelikans on the trip with me (the exception my soul sistah Joycie) the others wanted so badly for China to be like Disneyland *and I* loved the four empty baskets at the river crossing: I loved the exceptional inconvenience and abundance of unpredictability. I hated the spitting and unconscious nose-digging complemented by the boisterous burps. For the others, they had eaten too much fish, not enough napkins, diarrhea, and who wanted a menstrual period in China in those days?! The soldiers had to see everything in your luggage and you were the same age so you wanted to kick butt but it was only yours that could be targeted. Of course we were stared at constantly. You might even say, I even might have asked for it too. Remember the scarf and halter-top in the beginning? Well, I was much younger and prior to coming on the trip, I was dancing ballet and feeling oh so buff. Hell, it was summer and need I mention just how hot. Hot enough to wear cut-off jean shorts and the top part of my two piece bathing suit. Boiinng! went the eyes. Pppout went the old ladies lips. Up came the old scratch of the index finger on the cheek accompanied by the shaking head from side to side and the proper three-time tsk tsk tsk. I was an instant prostitute. I was a fool but the men and young boys could barely control their eyelids let alone their bodies which swaggered close to my own. Try to live in China for the summer and see how long you can last without having to resort to anything that could provide cool and maybe you too (if you are a woman) might turn your cotton scarf into a triangle and tie the flat long side behind your back so that when you stand on the ferry the cool breeze will be able to slip through the V part up between your breasts. The men get to stand barechested but this—and the top part of the two-pieced bathing suit—was all I could muster to keep cool. Unfortunately for the guys and Arnold the tour leader, I only turned the heat up.

Oh, the other thing I did in terms of costumes is that I have always loved those black old ladies high neck collars with side-seamed frogs. While we were in Zhongshan in the village visiting our ancestors or at least our relatives, I saw a lady wearing what I wanted and bought it off her back. Shit, talk about feeling like a high roller! Then, she produced an elegant one made of rayon. Whooowee, buy! I love those two black blouses—one for everyday fish catching; the other for special occasions. I could hardly contain myself when the two blouses were MINE. So to celebrate the event, I wore the cotton one to dinner with my white tennis shorts that night. Of course, no one could handle it. I was a contradiction in terms: butterfly bun, sexual white American style shorts, and horrors bent-back traditional grandma black blouse! Too much for the hundred of diners who had begun to find most of the sites a repeat. Here art was being brought to them in typical take-out style. Arnold almost fainted. Gary the junior guide's hair returned to its springy permanent curls and I took a slug of the famous warm beer.—If you ever go to China, be prepared to do a lot of drinking and sometimes what's there is only warm beer which hits the spot—you can feel the British conquering close by.

However, I suppose my true *pièce de resistance* is my crystal tortoise-framed round lens which Roberta the youngest high school grad in our group taught me how to get. "Just shove the cash in front of their faces and they'll take anything. Forget bargaining like a peasant." Gee, the kid knew such much more than I could have learned in this lifetime. So the glasses were MINE and I wore these glasses ev-erywhere. EVerybody looked at me like I was a lunatic because those were the Flash Dance days and everyone wanted to look so off the shoulder. I wanted to look like a class act. I wanted to at least look like my grandmother—ouuuuuuhh she was a knockout and I don't mean that I actually look like her nor does she have that flat classic look. No, grandma had the *guazi lian* look—the melon seed face. My cousin Pinky—if not for that beehive of curls around her beautiful face—has *that look*. Young or old, they are pretty (I think my cousin could be a danger if she ever pulled that hair back so that you could really REally see how pretty she is). So, I was happy in my bun to at least resemble grandma but those crystal lens were like drugs. Everything was upside down and when the car was moving, it was like bouncing from Neptune to Africa, New York and elsewhere. Then you'd be reminded that you were in China by the non-stop courteous two-timed honnk-honnkk bombarding from all moving wheels—cars, trucks, busses, bicycle bells, which at least were dainty; geese gobbling, chickens squawking, babies crying, and last but not least, the people famous for their worrisome frowns; they emitted an electricity that was ever so attractive. The temperature was cruel and the Chinese zither music was like a horse racing through my psyche. I was perfect for Shanghai. The Huangpu River, the Park Hotel, the Bund and European concessions had nothing on me, I was Cixi but prettier.

At night, I loved to walk the streets in my glasses. Then, it was safe; then, I was young and the world was at my impulse. I grabbed the moment and everything was adventure. Muscular and curious, I stooped and stopped at nothing. Then, it was safe. There, I was objectified. Nobody pulled the kind of stunts I invented. If you stayed inside the rooms, you had to set a lamp on the floor so the rats wouldn't run out, but outside there were people. In Nanchang, when it was hot, we'd hang out on the windows like everyone else in the city except that I wanted to send SOS signals to people who were watching us from their opposite buildings. So I flipped the lights on and off hoping Someone would respond. Of course Someone did, the security police issued an order to locate the persons attempting to create "art as I saw it" in the Russian-built hotel where we were staying. But in Shanghai, everyone was already bourgeois by 1983. People drank a lot already and were eager for anything foreign. Day and night on Nanjing Road, bamboo beds with people sleeping on them and vendors mixed. The human traffic was like the original twenty-four-hour Safeway. In Shanghai, the only difference is that, generally speaking, people dress a bit better because they are so conscious of how they look and they look like the cake in a Chinese bakery—sweet, tasty, and nearly just right. But I must include this prejudice against Shanghai people, they *are* a bunch of pimps imitating Western values with *un peu de vital élan*. Everyone in China knows that, including the Shanghainese, still I loved Shanghai because I had already been converted to Shanghai by way of Rita Nachman, who spent her childhood years there. And I loved Shirley—Miss Perfect—Nachman, the beautiful Rita's beautiful daughter who had these gorgeous red-embroidered silk pillow covers brought over to Amelika after the war. When I was in Shanghai, I wasn't Chinese for a moment, *I* was a Jewish Princess.

What did I like about *Zhong Guo*? My favorite place was and still is Tian'anmen Square because it's so damn big. There, you can breathe. There, you can be alone and think. And no park as I had expected, more like a giant concrete slab several state's worth of freeway. Herein lies something Chinese, and that is, No one can loiter in China. As the Chinese explain, in China no one can loiter because there's not enough space for anyone to be anywhere longer than for a few minutes—except at the train station where millions are waiting for Godot. There is simply not enough space for all humans and tourists combined (unless you move into the deserts or mountains of the Autonomous Regions), so the young boys in white uniforms called "police" come around to harass the people into continual movement—dance, if you will. And if want to sit, you cannot. There are no benches, and if you dare to squat which is common for many people in Asia, the police will glare at you to push on. Of course, if you are a foreigner, they bark and make hand gestures to giddy up or you'll be part of the round up. I love that place with a couple million twelve-inch squares on which humans crammed their bodies for Lao Mao or Uncle Mao's funeral. I love that place because it is the only place besides Hohhot in Mongolia where I felt private and therefore, free. Everything and everyone was neuter, and almost Daoist. You can really feel yourself as a particle in the great void. Numbers don't count because repression and oppression is cordially practiced as high art. Opinions don't matter because, after all, you're in the Middle Kingdom and where is that? but a state of mind. Wow! I love that place, mama. It is so fuckin metaphysical.

The cigarette smoke alone thick from the last four thousand years is a romantic intoxicant and then there was the taste of sweat.

Anything that was funky, I liked it. We all bought those Flying Nun white collapsible round hats which all the bicycle riders wore and looked like saintly road runners on the bicycles. I bought *de rigueur* soldier-green hat, pants, and jacket which have no labels because they are made at the labor reform camps, which is the Chinese poetic term for prisons. I bought cowboy boots in Mongolia with red, yellow, turquoise, and gold inlaid which all my travelling companions viewed as "too much" but then later regretted they didn't have the guts or fashion know-how to (once again) *buy*. I bought street lengths of brocade for my girls which they hated and only now ten years later appreciate. Of course, I bought jade: lavender fish and amber phoenix—hey those sound like names! I bought the most beautiful blue ink at the Summer Palace and several chops for me and the girls. My favorite is *Chang ge tiao wu*. "Singing and dancing" was what I thought I could live on for the rest of my life, heh heh. Oh, and I bought the Chinese version of high-top tennis shoes which were not meant to be comfortable just appear like the equivalent. And, you were constantly reminded of the country—at least on the surface—apologizing for "our country not so developed." Sometimes, however, when you don't have much, you treasure what you can get and do have. In China, *youpiao*, stamps are outrageously beautiful—oversized and romantic—and people horde 'em. You also loaded up on crackers because sometimes that was the only thing you'd dare eat. Once, we were at some mountain temple in some deep bamboo woods—who knows where—and actually quite lovely except that I had had my period that day and could only concentrate on where I could change my tampax in some private moment And hope that my supply could last the tour. Well, when it was chow time, there was an entire vegetarian meal set up for us in some pavilion with an army of flies attacking the food. You had to be there. Forget exotica, Li Bai, Bai Qiu Yi, and the T'ang dynasty. Crackers and polite smiling were enjoyed in the pavilion of flies deep in the humid woods. Last but not least, I bought my mosquito net which when I open up over my sweet quilt and sheets makes the person outside of the net feel like there's a princess inside and *that* must be me! Actually, it comes in handy when there is a mosquito whirriing around in the dark. And, I bought an original Bada Shangren in Nanchang. Do you know what "an original Bada Shangren" is boys and girls? The reason why I purposefully repeated the word "bought" is that the Chinese are so eager to know the price of everything and bargain in and around it. Not me; except for the glasses, I bought without lowering myself to shouting or negotiating. Finally, I had sex three times: first with a Chinese who came before entering the Jade Gates he was so excited. Then, I had sex in Mongolia with an Italian guy who sold zippers and clued me never to buy pants made in China with zippers because they were just beginning to make them and they always broke. Lucky me, he never got a hard-on. And there was the guide from Guangzhou who came inside his pants as he kissed me. Luckily my sex life improved on the next trip!

# How Chicano Philosophy Influenced Counter-Revolutionary Lau's Educating Immigrant Asians et al.

Why did I do It? I'll blame Arnoldo whom I hate anyway. I was in San Antonio teaching a workshop when Antoinette shows me something that the popular writer Arnoldo Garcia taught her how to make during his writing workshop.

What! my eyes blew fire! My library head condemned that stupid appropriator! How dare he take my culture and make art from it! My entire family was insulted! The whole Chinese race demanded revenge! I was jealous and thought I might do something similar after I re-educated Antoinette as to the damage Arnoldo accomplished when he *used* those sacred pieces of gold and silver newsprint and re-created art. The nerve! It bothered me for a long time until I was asked to do an art display at the airport with my young black blue brown green apple white and immigrant Asian babies. Sure, I'd do anything for fun. So I asked Lisa the teacher to check with the canon of culture, jolly and sexy Mrs. Pang, if we could use the gold and silver stuff for the art project and I don't know exactly what Mrs. Pang said to Lisa but Lisa took the hint that it wasn't such a swinging idea so we did bold Chinese characters instead. It didn't matter. I knew I was already in the process of creation, which had begun with making the buddah with three headless babies broken during the last earthquake as the focus of my Thanksgiving and Xmas altars.

That buddha was so fat and funny with all those bald babies crawling on his butt and shoulders, but when the earth quaked, it toppled from wherever it reigned and crack went the heads of the babies. It just looked like bad luck to adore a smiling buddha with perfectly healthy and well-dressed full bodies without heads. Enter the Disabilities Act, which confuses us not to call people headless, crippled, retarded, or sad sack. All of a sudden, my babies were contemporary: they had a rightful and dignified place. With dark glasses on, Buddha Man, which my younger daughter referred to as Mr. Nipples because he does possess some squeezables; with dried and perfumed flowers, candles, cans of pineapple labeled "Native Hawaiian"; *jalapeño* red and green pepper lights singing "Feliz Navidad" —a cigar wand of sage to offer now and then—the holidays seem to feel multicultural, definitely in sync with my psyche. And then Chinese New Year rolls around.

Well, I'm a dog, a god, a dog. Can I have any say so on how this year will be! A couple of days before blast-off, I walk across the street to Good Luck supermarket. Everyone is hoarding vegetables, meat, chicken and pork. I buy red candles, silver and gold paper, the gold stuff with the blood-red stamp. I buy two *feng shui*—send the bad spirits away mirrors, red paper with gold cuts that say "money, money; money in the afterlife pays dentist bills for bad teeth; can buy another wife or all the husbands you want; money makes happy." I also bought some incense and a pack of Bank Notes for Hell, which only come in ten-thousand-dollar denominations. I was set.

The Next Day. The next day, I hauled my party favors to school for fun. First I show the kids what I have brought and ask them if they know what it is. Right away all the Cantonese speakers erupt in pentatonic thrill knowing what I have brought. The Chinese Mericans, the Vietnamese, Cambodians, Blacks, and Latinos know that this is yet another subtle test to show Who knows What in this heavily-populated Asian school in Oakland's Chinatown. Their wide and long eyes are taut. Their mouths form questions.

"Ouuu, Aunty Lau brought play money," says Echo, one of my favorites, who looks like my own half-white, some-Hawaiian-and-Chinese daughters when they were babies.

"That's not play money," scolds Charles who is from China. "It's money for the dead. You have to burn it," he frowns.

"Aunty Lau, isn't that play money?" pleas the little girl.

"It's play for me," I announce.

The Cantonese speakers are fascinated and frightened that Aunty Lau has brought in all these bright colors as if they were toys, which they know are meant to be burned for the dead ancestors. Why has Aunty Lau created anarchy in the classroom? Blame Mildred the Terminator (cannot keep her spirit or body down too long) my mother who for years rolled the paper into gold, silver, and gold with red ingots to be for family members—wherever. Blame her, the sisters, and aunts who groaned about rolling those mothers—the backaches from sitting and rolling for what? Since the next generation of troops are not in sight, the Carriers of Culture might as well roll enough for themselves for when they're dead And manufacture robots who would then burn the ingots for their dedicated "passed spirits." And they were always interrupted in their rolling if they were *lah tsah*, if they were dirty because they were menstruating; if it was raining. Or, they couldn't roll during the night. There are other conditions but I don't want to remember them: it was enough for me to decide that it was beyond time that guys start investing in this ritual. What period would stop a guy from dedicating a few hours to his ancestors? Guys outshine women as chefs, hair stylists, writers—everything—let the guys make gold from paper.

The little kids all loved the idea. After I showed them how to make gold from paper, lockstep we all made some. The Chinese teacher from China never made any in her life. The Chinese Merican teacher born in Oakland never rolled any. How did Aunty Lau know this secret stuff? We needed assistance and luckily a hunky of a Chinese male was scheduled to work with the kindergartners.

Danny from Hong Kong *knew* that this was exclusive women's work but Danny's work in the classroom was to assist the teachers, so thirty-something Danny rolled his first gold ingot and taught other kids how to make them also. But are kids—even Chinese kids—really interested in gold? Of course not. They constructed baby cradles and rocked imaginary dolls in their arms. They spied at each other in their tele/periscopes. Super-typically Hong Kong, they yakked Cantonese into their cellular telephones. They made hats and bridges, boats and burritos. They made fun. They changed the New Year. The dogs were barking and licking their imaginations. The gods were naked and enjoying themselves for a change. Mrs. Pang almost fainted when she passed the class and saw the kids testifying to make more art in the Year of the Dog instead of more A's or more money. Later, on the street while we passed each other doing our market strut she hailed me down to ask, "Are you going to burn the gold paper?"

"Burn it? No, I'm making an altar at home and I'm adding chocolate hearts because Valentine's Day is coming up."

Her eyes floated in wonderment as if to sigh "That Miss Lau, always making trouble," and we smiled full smiles at each other; her, happy and lucky not to be me, and me, I said, "Mrs. Pang, you are carrying two bags of food. Look what I'm carrying? a bag full of narcissus bulbs. Some people like to have food, I like to have flowers."

"That's okay Miss Lau," she replied, "you happy. That's all that matters."

Later that night I phone my mother who has adjusted to my wired art ways. I tell her the whole story and expect she will scold me at some point which she doesn't do and even adds that

"Children are so delightful in their imagination."

I tell her that I have burned a few of the gold bricks but perhaps at eighty-seven she doesn't care and agrees that I am not so important nor powerful enough to offend anyone. The kids were happy. My mother and I were happy. It was Chinese New Year and just another day in Amelika. One of the Chinese teachers had on new red shoes. Mrs. Pang had a new perm.

The next day I went and had auburn streaks installed in my scalp. Somebody asked if I had had Chinese New Year's dinner.

Nobody invited me. I didn't want to eat it. My younger daughter was in Washington. My husband was out chasing me and some traditions get fooled into becoming well-respected albatrosses while others get in the way of artists. These are the lucky ones: Staying Alive, staying alive. Bloody in birth, stinging their everlasting magic (they are) waking/shaking up living and dead.

*Hui Shenma bu?* Why not!

# From the Diary of *Bu Yau Shu Cai* or A Translation from the Ancient Secrets of Forbidden Fruits

## by *I Qi Xiao Jie*

Well, I never had sex with an Asian American and *Tian ah*, heaven forbid that ever happens! I'm old-fashion Chinese woman. I like to hear my lovers swoon bits of opera in Chinese. I don't want to hear "Oh baby, it feels soo good." I demand stones move in battles. I treasure galloping horses and chariots with whips—gimme a Chinese man with a title. Butcher is good. Cadre is common. A watchmaker can promise an orgasm every day at five o'clock after he closes the shop. A paleontologist can promise romance into the past, but if he urges you to square off on the grid lines so he can measure your tail or mouth you'd better be the type that enjoys eating bitter melon. Once I had a semiotician for a lover. Oh, he was so jealous. I couldn't powder my skin or twirl my neck in the breeze without him interpreting my gestures as erotic or perverse. And I was forced to speak in English to him. When it was time for us to challenge our wits skin to skin, I refused to roll out the golden carpet for him. I shrieked and moaned in Chinese. I never said "Fuck me, baby" in English. No, I was a rotting melon with him: he liked the calamity. Skinny and nearly blind, till this day I'm amazed how crazy I was for his tin cannon, but he was smart. Really, I didn't need anyone else to discuss the matter of consequence. He was so smart and could reference everything in at least four languages. That was scholar Deng who was replaced by Electrician Chin.

There was Lao Ma who slanted his eye like sharks and claimed me as his "gi pu si"—his "Gypsy sweetheart." And the taxi-driver recited great poetry and gave me splendid gifts. Big and always on time. Boast about fast—he could change money in a flash. Dirty money, foreign exchange, good black-market prices. Oh yes, how could I forget the zookeeper who smelled like thousand-year-old eggs and panted hopping off his bicycle as he wagged to my compound. Mr. Zhang who was married to the doctor and only spoke Japanese would courteously smile at me while we stumbled over my debts. And, I would wage my family property that Mr. Li is so happy that we no longer share the same compound: when he "promised" to correct the error in the lease agreement and made no attempt, oh, it was a tragedy in translation and pretension.

I remember the day distinctly when Chan Dayi, my favorite gatekeeper, had been stonily happy and Mr. Li had inquired if some good luck had come the old man's way. Chan Dayi mentioned that Lady Shu had returned from abroad and Mr. Li, anxious to show off his new learned skills in English paid me a visit soon thereafter. To impress me, the old dunce spoke to me entirely in English and further carved a place for himself among farm animals by "promising" to secure a favorable lease agreement among the peasants who worked my father's land in Anhui Province. Tobacco is fast becoming the new industry in my country so it is fitting that all documents be executed immediately. Well, twenty-four hours passed and, rightly so, the man could have been skinned alive in public or even in private before his family. I, however, approached him directly—American style as he approached me. Scared chicken as he was, what a pity such a good-looking fool made entirely of himself. The whole town trailed him and because he had worked for the *Wai Ban*. The people in the German, French, English, and Italian concessions all were wagging and chortling behind his back—and in their own language, to his face ridiculed Li's foppery and Lady Shu's daredevil begging for justice. Eventually, the matter was taken care of and Mr. Li could once again open up his big mouth, sting you with his bad breath and brag.

Unfortunately, life goes on. Only last week I was seated at the same table as Republican Liu, who reminded me of Zhao the Gambler. Idiot that he is, Zhao is as common as any character in the works of the famous Tianjin writer. Briefly, there was an incident with a dissident, and the other dissident—the mechanical engineer, his wife, and son, which as a result, I hold title of MFS—Most Favored Sister. The relationship with my brother-in-law with thick glasses is extremely covert: he likes gospel music, the tango, and me at a distance. There was Dr. Shrimp the plumber and Mr. Jiang the window man who used to wear a DKNY shirt his daughter sent him from a used clothing store in America.

I especially remember the gentleman at the Summer Palace wearing the wide-brim straw hat who sat cross-legged with a stone pillow beneath his feet created in the old way just for comfort. In 1983, you could still find those signs but the tourists have destroyed everything small and big. The gentleman reminded me of my mother's father who came from a good family but like all of us lost his money to his greed. Gaunt and tall like all Northerners, you knew he was a ghost from the past mediating the past with the present not even approaching future as he was still reconciling the past with the ancient past in the scholarly way. Black briefcase to the side, he sat under a cassia tree in full bloom, the blossoms fragrance steamy in the Beijing heat. Textbook case, one moment he was millions of broken porcelain pieces among the gravel and grass unnoticed in the porcelain cities like Jingdezhen. As I noticed this artifact without betraying him, I scribbled a few lines in the cuff of my sleeve, which caused my stupid maid servant to gasp. Immediately, it was over. With their weighty and strange-smelling body odors, the tourists packed upon my life like vultures with their many shapes of camera. The gentleman and I became as dirty as the Huangpu River, common as all smiling wooden buddhas. So what, we cannot be Chinese forever I guess.

Before my husband, I used to believe that I loved dreaming about the paleon-tologist the most. Just dropping his title raised my position. How many people are linked with a "paleontologist"? And, he was a high official too. I remember requesting a photo of him properly smoking a cigarette when out in the fields of Yuanmou. Then, I didn't know he didn't smoke and the fire hazard was risky when he lit up nested in the dry grasses, only later to be dubbed by my colleagues in America "The Marlboro Man." God, he was good-looking. Tall, confident—the mustache is what hooked me. None of these Americanized versions of yellow Ken, partner to Barbie. Couldn't speak a word of English fortunately! High forehead, cheekbones like guarding lions; could travel abroad easily; with a driver; many keys and special privileges; plus, the wormiest cannon in four thousand years of Chinese history. No problem with *kou jiao* therefore; as well, no challenge. We all shrivel and fade as we get old, don't we? Crags and rivers as he was, when I last saw him during Mid-Autumn Festival, he looked like a has-been *and* had convinced himself that I still was the foolish school girl that he was introduced to by nature. No, just because my husband was not visiting the capitol with me did not mean that my legs were fast noodles ready to be boiled. *Tai tsou le,* it was over.

Speaking of *kou jiao*, it is engraved on the family's ancient female seal that "To eat persimmon is like eating woman." "Chi shi zi xiang chi nu zi." The other saying goes "A mouthful of won ton or *shui jiao* is good-eating cunt." Since this closely guarded family proverb is still banned in China, try to use your imagination for this translation because I cannot provide it. My male cousin is a female partner to a very high official and the official could lose face if a translation is produced. Nonetheless, I was relieved for the deliverance of that rain drop of a cannon because I have a classic beauty's mouth: a red dot, no more. And my gatekeeper whom I dearly miss created the smallest and most delicious *jiao zi* on all earth for my mouth so that it need not stretch nor shove nor shift to accommodate the delicacy. One day, when I was swallowing herbs for my well-known charm, it occurred to me that I had difficulty swallowing the potions. Well, lightning struck my intellect and I resolved that how could I swallow my young husband's too-big cannon if I could barely swallow the smooth capsules of charm? This was a question for my mother, my soul's inspiration.

When mother was visiting a month ago and I was in the East Wing taking my charm potions, as usual, the discomfort of taking the herbs forced me to complain.

"These big chucks are hard to swallow. It's like having oral sex." My mother slapped her knee and frowned. Then, I began to choke and burp.

"What's your problem?" She remarked.

"I told you. This medicine is like oral sex." Again, she slapped her knee indignantly. But when I continued to burp, she curiously turned and whispered "What's matter, mouth too small?"

My mother has a special language with my Chinaspecial: she is constantly reminding me that I don't appreciate Him, Mr. Big and Yummy Cannon, my husband.

"Look at the new roof. Twenty double-paned new windows. You don't appreciate anything."

I swooned, "I did appreciate them in December. I don't appreciate them now. He's so firm. He's so tall. He's so bad. He's so cute, I want him to love me."

"The problem with you is that you're just itchy down there all the time." Yup, that's what my mama told me.

When the government requested that I write a special article on the Education of Youth Regarding *Kou Jiao*, I was so alarmed. Such responsibility, such a privilege! What research it would entail and what nightmare experiences I only had. It was time to consult Ah Fut. Poor scholar Fut. A longtime companion who had practiced English with me for many many years, he knew all the secrets. In Chinese, he was known as a Piggyback, also known as a Crossover. Born in Kaifeng to a Jewish mother and a Chinese father, he was raised in Shanghai in the Jewish concession after his mother was forced to seek refuge from his father who required that his mother perform the famous ancient Animal Acts named after a monkey master. Then, it was still common practice among scholars to insist that their wives devote their bodies to the Art of the Oyster or the very tragic Art of the Anteater. The Art of the Frog was most humorous but it was the Art of the Turtle that shocked scholar Fut's talkative mother into silence. Gossip believed that the old man planned it that way so that he could then practice Traveling Lotus and Dangling Cold without question or correction by his loving but not exactly erotic wife. There is an old Chinese saying, "A son's cannon is stretched by his father's digging." Of course, this does not travel well once transferred into English, but scholar Fut and I sobbed many evenings into the next sunrise desperate to rearrange the gamut of his metal cannon. Disguised as monks we ransacked all the best gardens for panda eye drops, wisteria pollen, and royal peanut jelly. In those days, I was a slave to any human failure and scholar Fut was an embarrassment. Fast with words, bald, big eyes, he sometimes snorted but he could never produce an heir. One day while dredging his bad luck over noodles, I overheard some foreigners brag about the benefits of something called oral sex! On fire with the danger of these new thrills, I conveyed the concept to Ah Fut, who nearly fainted. Upon finishing our order, we bullied out of the noodle house to strategize on how we might locate the candidate who could most flatter Ah Fut with this new trick. If he wasn't so picky, I would have tried to be the first myself, but deprived as he was; recovering from his long attachment to his former mistress Lady Mangoes; and given his talent for biting, I offered the occasion to another beauty. *Ai ya!* when it was over, he told me in detail how much oral sex rescued his soul and that rather than pursue the production of an heir, he preferred to spread his thighs like a walrus and forget he was human!

*Poi!* my daughters and I had very long chats about the subject and while squatting in the public toilets one afternoon, my younger daughter Lightning Intellect clued me in that just because I supposedly have a difficult time with oral sex, I was not the universal measurement—that every woman in the universe did not encounter lock jaw; broken lip tissue from teeth bearing down upon the lips; and worst, the addiction for more cannon shooting available around the clock whenever my gates of heaven desired—when challanged with the near occasion of oral sex. Another time, my older daughter offered that my own saintly mother probably did it with my father because he was from Xinjiang and it is well known that the Chinese from Xinjiang are truly Turks. Peony Eyes also remarked that probably her grandmother didn't initiate anything, but that she probably went along because grandfather seduced her analytic mind with some powerful delivery of forbidden fruits.

With that ammunition, I was determined that when my mother next came to visit, I would kindly solicit her comments on the history of her own sex life, but when I tried vigorously, she stamped her tiny foot to the floor. As the very last opportunity, while accompanying mother to the city gate, I tried once more only to miss the right road and wind up in a narrow alley. Undaunted, mother rolled her eyeballs as though pleading for father to release her from my taunts. Sighing (in the classic manner), we patted each other's back, kissed, and turned.

When my husband returned from the capitol, I wanted to fill his ear with my silly wisdom but no. I boiled the corn that he brought as gifts. We ate the flame white peaches without skins. We sat side by side not quite knowing what to say to each other. It had been so long since I had last smelled the corners of his body in his clothes or seen the thickness of his wrists. His fingernails need to be clipped. He was as handsome as ever. Bold and as deep in his pain as when I first felt his presence, he was still sick, coughing and sneezing: one day he was home, the next day he was off to another city. Today, he was home to look at me and not touch. And then, briefly, he angled his arm like a hook through my neck. All I needed. My raw and clever man. I took a deep breath and swore loyalty to him.

Politely in the classic Chinese way, not looking at him, I praised him saying "I love you"

"I love you" says my China husband. "You don't know how painful, it is." And he's right, I don't know and most of the time, I was so busy practicing English, I was beginning to be English—not just American, but that stinky kind of Hong Kong English, the worst kind.

Will I remember any good behavior? Lying before me, my husband is the feast of the ocean's undertow—bounty of sea cucumber, oysters, and clams. In the surf's passions, I dive into unknown chants wave after wave. China husband and I are here—or there in the void; earth not essential. Only the need to prolong wanting; to sustain rub. Without the end, it's nothing, but not yet. Don't. Without dream, earth has no appeal; too much, scandalous. His dark nipples asleep, my peach man could pass for any two-legged chinaman. But those thighs; that collection of brain, volcanic and sweetly welcoming—confronts and contracts danger which is *necessary* for healthy sex. His springtime voice when he's in a good mood; his private clown manners; Beijing opera in my own life—how could I have interest in any other mortal after my own valiant version of Ah Q?

It is twenty days and my husband is floating among the stars and sirens. Where is he? A common American man would be beached on the sofa watching the television as my husband practiced when he was not strangled by his business. Perhaps when he returns, I can recite the new words in English I have learned from the literary magazines, which include "fuck you," "donkey penis," and of course, "mouth with dumpling inside." I will discuss the subject of oral sex detailed in formal and official Chinese. English, of course is merely my business language. Someday, I will embroider the pleasures of Nine Mountains and Snow

Rivers on silk in order that the government may have their auspicious report on reference. As ideals seem to disappear and new ones become substitute for good taste, I presume that within a few years my grandchildren might challenge each other on the best examples of oral sex.

Anything can happen today.
What can a woman do?

Meanwhile, I am refining some aspects of the policy—a lot of work—and I continue to interview foreigners. It is rather amazing that I am required to submit such a report; however, science is science. Duty is duty. We Chinese have a long history proving our diligence to duty. Soon though, soon, the report shall be in order.

Bio Note: *I Qi Xiao Jie* is the name of a good Chinese wife.

# 4

## *Ka Mea Ka Mea, Ei Nei*—Sweetie, where you stay?

### The Man (White man) Who Got Away—
### after some strong urging on my part

I decided that I had to write about S especially because he had the same name as my eventually-to-be-former husband. How did it happen? My Steve was in China and I hadn't heard from him in a month. I didn't know if he was dead, in prison, or what. My then not so good friend Susan recommended this bow-tie type as a possible date for me, and me with no life considered the long Memorial Day weekend and what would I fill in the blanks as to my "activities" when my mother would call to see if I was like everyone else? I knew I would barbeque with Abdou on Saturday and I would go to Carnival with Professor Zhang—there was an emptiness of this three-day weekend when all the regular humans would run away or at least stroll hand-in-hand somewhere, so when the possibility of going to Davis Hall popped up, "Oh, I can finally wear my Kenneth Cole shoes that I bought in April! And, I can see if I still know how to put on eyeliner" suggested that it *might* be worth it, I threw the towel in.

Well, he called me to have a voice and brain check and it went okay. I suggested that if we hated each other, I could just come home after the concert, which he was reaaallly loOking forward to. Not me, really. When I was in college and super into all things European—the whole Greco-Roman thang: the myths, the archetypes; Jung and the twenty plenty Bollingen series on symbols *especial*, the Apollonian Dionysian Duality; not just a little bit but All of Rilke, Schopenhauer, Heidegger, Nietzsche, Goethe, and Neumann (did I and still do love Neumann—*achtung*)—I'm tired of remembering/I don't want to *exert* myself. There was also Kachaturaian et al. (I know he's not German; think "college," man), Mahler among. I Am Not a Mahler fan. He is okay if you are a dull type, but epiphany, hell no, not Mahler.—How about *The Origin of Consciousness in the Breakdown of the Bicameral Mind*—wasn't that a hot item, I think I'll pull it out as winter meditation. But I was willing to be well-behaved—all those years of ballet and self-restraint followed by years of *adagio avec porter bras*. Bottom line, I figured that if it was a bust, I could (as history has proven) write about it.

Well, the eyeliner went on easeee as grease. I had a chance to suede-proof my new Ken Coles.

What can I say? I looked the way Amy Tan would want to look. Unfortunately for me, Amy Tan knows how to behave much better than I. In my imagination, I may have written that I could have looked like her but I eventually behaved like Kamapua'a instead.—Thank god for Tita Lo Mouth as the objectified icon. *Akua* knows I don't agree with almost everything she says and does, but I can at least use her as a reference of "culture" this or that. Anyways, when this guy comes purposefully marching up
to my *hale*, I know this is yet another (mis)adventure.

"Hello"
"Hello" and we were off on a Friday late afternoon onto the Bay Bridge, in traffic like most
humans at that time but this guy says to me
"Do you love music?"
I'm thinking "Do I (fucking) *love*? music?"
Now what kind of a stupid (fuck) question is that?
Do I *love* music?
Would I fuck music?
Would I run off to China with music?
Would I chase music not knowing whether I could make a life of it?
Do I "love" music?
Is that the first question?
No introductory "great day," "I'm glad the traffic's moving," "How was your day today?"
How about something more friendly, like—"What kind of music do you like?"

Howsabout starting off with "like" instead of "love"?
This guy and his bow tie were way off the bull's ass, but maybe I was wrong!
Maybe everybody else in their cars and
everybody in the Bay Area and
everybody in California—
maybe the whole world was having this same conversation at that very moment
But maybe I was the only fool not to be on the great superhighway
Maybe I was still on earth wearing my eyeliner, black Jockey panty hose, and
see-through vision
Maybe I didn't appreciate highbrow pre-Mahler lecture small talk.

Eh, we made it to the City. He found a parking space and pulled out that damn
"the club," which irritated me when I saw him unlock his petty solid grey Honda
as I first got in. Then, we bustled to Davis Hall—the air summer crisp (don't
you hate how white people talk like this, "mah-va-l,ous" "fah-bu-lous"—the
concept originating in the throat to the nostrils into the eyeballs with the lids
partially drooping darting through the skull mixing with the rest of the hot air
overhead). Eh, I'm glad I went: to get a reality check. I hate the symbol of the
symphony—bastion of white whiter whitest whiteout. If I could take a quilt
and fall asleep listening to Mozart, Brahms, Vivaldi, and one or two Beethoven,
that would be humane and I might even donate money to the symphony, but
stiff back; clearing throats and noses only between movements—what the fuck
kind of life is that? If I have to speak or write passing English I can, and even, on
rare occasions, be titillated in English, but to cultivate myself for the rest of my
life in Euro-cult, no tanks eh. Everybody knows that even Prince Charles has
politely proven that he's no snob on earth. It's just dress-up for him everyday.
Don't we know from Charlie that this is all fruit punch anyway?

So, we're sitting listening to this "enlightening" crap before the concert and my
date cups his hand and whispers that Mahler's wife was a "prize."
"Prize? Prize?"
Much later he explains his sardonic humor that infact, she was "difficult."
I can really tell that this guy don't speak no T(h)ird Worl(d) lingo. This guy like
consonants. He like bite. Why he's chewed so many words there's a little arch
carved into his two front teeth that makes him look like a cross between Alan
Alda and Dracula. Deep breaths time.
Thank god, the lecture is over and we get a chance to fart silently beneath our
gowns and tight lips. We do the white thing and "get a drink." In our case
because we're *tres polite*, we get a glass of Chardonnay. Not the way he likes it:

*tres froid. Pas mal.* It's only to loosen him up but he doesn't realize that this ain't no *lūʻau.* An then, the ring ting ting-ling of the golden bells charming us hither to music.

An uninterrupted hour of what? No soul. No love. A lot of head sounds which whites justify as "excellence." I was glad it was over when it finally was. So he asked if I would like a bite to eat. Now who eats that late? You know the answer: white people. Of course, I was willing to be white people for a day. Where should we dine? How about on the other side of the Bridge, I suggest (the run home is closer; the taxi fare cheaper).
We go somewhere in Emeryville and share a sandwich and another glass of wine. Now, I'm in trouble: now, he's getting interested in me. Oh, I'm flattered that my old slap in the face attitude can still attract a guy with money, but I've had enough. I'm ready for the boredom that is my current lifestyle. *Non, non, non. En route chez moi*, he steadily tires me into agreeing to have yet one more glass of wine. All right all right. We go to a jazz club in my neighborhood. The music sounds like a marching band but I really don't care: I can tell my mother that I went to the symphony and I'll be home between my flannel sheets soon enough.

And then, it's time to go: and then I'm there at my house. Thank god my kid has friends over making loud noise. I shake his hand and say "Thank you and good night." When the kids hear me unlock the door, they are silent. When I sleuth in past twelve they scold, "Where have you been? It's after twelve!" At forty-eight, fat and a failure, I don't need to answer.

THE DAYS AFTER:
He's calling all the time. I feel like Zorba the Greek but that image is wrong. Yesterday, while lying in bed, the entire chant came to me and I can't reproduce it but more or less I feel like I'm part of a sound
part of atoms in a fiber
sometimes part of me is the hummm in an everlasting wave
If you are used to diagramming sentences or divide life into boxes
you'll have a difficulty believing me: it's foreign
which is why we have the word *hā-ole*, without breath
—I like handkerchiefs and kleenex. I'm glad white man invented that—
but brown people are the mud: we're dirt and ash elements of this here, this now

we're also from the past and in the future. *Nothing* controls this rhythm
but how the white man tries—yellow man too, I think.
Brown folks are roots and trunks and branches of the earth.
We are the owls and sharks and rocks and lizards.
Our voice is an eternity echo which makes little magic in English
This generation is the first to speak in a clear rhythm of earth because
finally, we breathe from our own sounds, our physical wisdom gathered in
prayer
to guide us in our earth and skyways by blood or by spirit
all sewn together by this Rhythm Which Nothing Controls
Who dares to lead the Rhythm Which Nothing Controls?

this was not the chant at all, but it felt close to it. That's because the Rhythm is
today and today's chant is different from yesterday.

But the guy—gee, I never had a chance to figure out if he was nice or not. He had
too much time and was impatient. I was kinda interested in him. I mean, when
he invited me to come over for a glass of wine and I stepped into his pad—I
mean, it was not Versailles but nice furniture, nice dinnerware, nice table and
chairs. I gripped myself and noted, "Aye, you can be li 'dis" (translation: you
Carolyn can certainly pretend to be your old high school self), "I'm a candidate
for this place." And when Susan and Fred came over, I even enjoyed myself
briefly but then they all drank too much of that lovely wine. Well, I called
home and Ana had had a nosebleed at work; the paramedics had arrived and it
was time to go. Now (gotta admit) it feels reassuring he didn't want me to leave
but he was too much too soon too fast.

Next thing you know, he's saying he wanted to nominate my friend Susan for
the Nobel Prize of Love.
Next thing you know, he's promising to take me to the Black and White Ball
Next thing you know, he's going to take me to live in France
Next thing you know, he's "suggesting" where I would make copies in his
neighborhood
Next thing you know, we're in Chinatown where he's never been before and
doesn't know how to behave with me
Next, he's asking me "Why do you drink that stuff?" meaning Coke and offering
me Trader Joe's "wonderful" chips that remind me of cow shit
When I let him kiss me—just a little—the id **S**o *ono* fo some ting, id says

Aye, go catch one wave
wen's the last time, eh?
go wipe out, brah

and da Republican Hawaiian superego dainty in all its purveyances of protocol
frowns

BUT what about his breath dahling?
what? the *ma'i lele* so itchy, you can close down da nose and mout?
that breath sweetheart, that breath is soo—like bitta and stale an lita bit
sau-wa

and my own prissy body that melts to the smell of fresh-cut grass which reminds
me of watermelon and contracts to the crank odor of too much ampit—I
KKkcaNot stand up to BO and BB. No need say mo.—Aye how's about when
you see one rich kind tight permanent wave lady or a teacha or somtimes people
like tell you someting on da sly, like Real quiet, eh, and they bring deir mout
ever so discreetly into your nose range

Ai! Kadayu as my daddy would wince

You know when you go down da beach and get da kine signs say

**WARNING!**
**NO SWIMMING ALLOWED**
**DANGEROUS UNDERTOW**
(Yor mudda goin pull your hair if she finds out
Yor fadda, yor fadda goin geeeve you lih-kin
Aye, stupid, you like try?)

I guess this is my invisible placard because I get as nasty as that breath and
body that stink if it Proceeds to AtTempt to *engage* in civil behavior as though
the earth were in perfect harmony.

Then he's calling me all the time while my mother and cousins are visiting
because Ana is going to graduate from high school

One time when he calls, da buggah got the nerve, The NERVE to "share" that he "wants to bite" me.

Bite me?

Bite your ass

Now where did this *haole* imagine that he, *l'estrangeur*, was going to be privileged to bite me?

What gave him any indication that I was the wanting-to-be-bitten acolyte?

Bite me? what I look like one pok chop?

Bite me? B-i-t-e me? Me? be-ing bitten by mosquito is bad enough. Being bitten by a bee is bad. Flea bites are a pain in the ass. A puppy bite with those "innocent" sharp teeth are what you get when you get one puppy. The last thing that bit me was that damn Smokey, Ana's lopped-ear rabbit Whom I allowed to live in the living room so she could see the outdoor forest through the picture window. No matter that Smokey was allowed to ruin the hardwood floors. She was treated like everyone else in this house, and one day while Ana was letting her leap in the house And I was lying on the floor, Smokey leaped onto my chest and bit my nipple. It was not fun-ny. So being bitten by a human was a worrisome departure from my last indignant encounter with being bitten. Separately, the last reference of human biting that I could recall was Jeffrey Dahmer. So when this fool who only liked classical music and jazz; whose first piece of writing he is submitting to the Smithsonian; who washes the fruit from Berkeley Bowl and towel-dries it before displaying it in the dining room; *Qui est Monsieur Passe Simple arrive*: heh heh heh, eh

And he calls three times one night while I'm out babysitting Professor Zhang, who has begged me to accompany him to the City to see his *hao pengyou* Allen Ginsberg who (news to me) turns out to be *en charmant*

Now I'm beginning to believe that I have a stalker on my hands

Now, I'm more that irritated: now I'm not so well liked, loved, or adored

Now he has to watch out: he has touched my nerves

my unpopular nerve, my pagan logic, my survival instinct—if I inhale deeply and

just trust my ancestors, a gesture so unique, it always responds to my deepest wish:

what lesson from my ancestral resources perform in the clearest truth?

I call him on the telephone and he's sulky. No matter. I am just a messenger. He's whining. No matter. All I have to do is be calm and convey the teachings. Finally it's time so I say

I   will   eat   the white man's food
and I   will pray   to the white man's god   but
I'm   not too eager   about whitemen
and   it's   going   to be   a long time   before
my sheets   smell like   white man.

So when he didn't know what to say, then I really wanted to bust him up.
Oh, he was sorry that he "couldn't be as glib" as me.
Then, I told him that I felt sorry for him because he didn't know how to be like
one of us: didn't know how to roll with the punches. I dunno, it's a story, eh. I
saw him once after that.
Everybody was smoking dope except him. I never smoke dope anymore, but
that day I did while schmoozy-whoozing with the artistes. Then, I left when
they continued to drink and my friend's head was in the toilet. Thank myself
I live a few minutes away. Then one day, I called him up to ask if he'd like
coffee—oh, he was "busy writing." Man, these kind writers—s'why hard, eh.
Now, months later, I called him up, said I was writing about the time when
I knew him—told Lily that I was doing it for the narrative—and she made a
suggestion but I ignored her.
So I left a message
Then, he called when I was on the phone and I said I'd call him back then he
called back while I was still on the phone with Lily to announce that he was
going out and would speak to me tomorrow.
Well, it's tomorrow and his call interrupts while I'm talking to my friend and I
say that I'll call back.
Later when I call back, it's the machine again so I politely leave a message that
I called.

Here's the punch line: when he calls back—and you know he will—I'll have to
break the news to him that I'm done. Let's see him make pasta outa poop. He
reminds me of my Blaund from Blaunder Old friend. A little white blood, not
so bad but too much east coast white blood—ahhh *pilikia*
Dose blue-eyed blonds and supposed rare combinations of black and blue like
Dick when he was young, *haole* guys
*haole* guys wit deir elevated kind cultcha—
wha? doo dey know!

*WHAT?* do *haole* really know

# The IdealMAN in the Matches Column:
# Will You Be My Matinee Idol?

**It** started out as an innocent lunch—one that we've "done" before. Allways civil and comfortable, We always manage to get Ozu Kawabata into the conversation. I: am always grateful I canfeel "the range of possibilities" with This guy—may I quote myself? as if I were nominating the candidate a benefit of "having the *capacity* of 'the range of possibilities.' " Inevitably *the guy* rots into mediocrity or at perhaps short of, but simply not in touch with, the demands of qualifying as a human being in these times.

Yes. Yes, Yesterday, was it the angle of autumn's light creeping under my short and revealing skirt?
Was the tone of his voice like Little Bear's *just right* porridge, chair, and bed so that while listening to Weil or saxaphone or Hawaiian or Cubana rap,
Or the *just right* timing of him (after purchasing two CD's) *and* returning to Krishna where I
was copying text to locate the perfect publisher—
or maybe the *near right* calculation of how much the copies totaled–
it could've been the Right seafood panfried noodles at the Yellow Emperor Club in Emeryville

and/or but all the words and movements and books and steps and sweet rhythm that were taxing my estrogen and progesterone, I felt like a persimmon ripening and between green, semi-orange, and breast-ripe, all I could do was ripple along until I was cutting green onions—or icons later.

Hours later, a flu warmed me.
The healthy me, the one before lunch, was nowhere. I really knew:
I loved him. I knew it because I feel shy.
Of course no one would believe I could be shy, or grateful that I never chose to or was unRestrained in my earlier sniff towards *other*.
(my dress skirt uplifted, the grass green one with eyelets)
Now I can love him. Now he can love me—ineach our own conventionally comfortable way. Maybe from his house where maybe he will build more than More bookcases after he knows: because I will love him through text where we both reside.

Perhaps I will reveal myself under the "s" of "skin"—what a fancy idea! Probably I will hide inside the ridges of trees and glottal stops. Glottalia are my current rage.

HE is Not like the other white guys: I've had eight years to watch him. I like that he likes slow and is very fast in that slowness. Generally, humans come in two modes; fast or slow. I know I *appear* slow but only because I am figuring out the angle from which to "reply," "behave," "perform," "proceed." I talk less and less these days because people only want to hear their opinions reflected in their ears.

Most verbal exchange prevails in the land of "How much?" or "Go away":
"How much can you give me?"
"Go away, you're not giving me what I want."
"You don't give me Enough. Go."
Race per race, gender to gender, this the common language. Some races take more time between the "how much?" and "go away" part, but when the "how" and "much" fail to coordinate, the "go away" is sure to kick in.
Norm is not like that. Norm's language are different steps in a dance. Maybe that's how I was soothed by his voice, slow but considerate placement of ideas. There are places for me to lie and see the stars through the ceiling into the daylight sky. I can run upstairs into his mind and slide down with my bra strap showing. Even when he mispronounces "Qi" (chee), volunteering the understandable "key" in a Chinese name, he is monsieur señor avec matinee idol *internationale*. And he sings a title of song.
—No
rm, were you always This way? or has it taken me so long to pay attention to you? Or maybe, I dunno.
—Could it be that you're like this with everyone and you have armies of Norm admirers? (Together I feel) We're so AWARE with each other—is it because language and movement transfer Something to us?
Or, have we simply always liked each other? Liking someone a little over a long time is a lot of unnoticeable pluses. And one day—or perhaps, lingering in remnants of the day after, suddenly while washing dishes, one Needs to hear Luther Vandross oozing through the arches of your feet up the calves sweeping the pelvis onto the shoulder until *finalement*, the subject, verb, and you the direct object of desire—or you, predicate adjective feel that youthful dizzy glow of hormones zapping each breath and staring outside beyond the window, *c'est vrai*! You love him, or is it he loves you? Did he trick you? did he love me first?

[—what if Norm has a boyfriend? Norm could already have a boyfriend and a girlfriend. He could have boyfriends; he could have girlfriends too. Norm, you know I can't deal with that]

It is time to pick some flowers and gently chant the eternal question: he loves me, he loves me not.
God, I hope he loves me: could my tiny breasts be so Wrong? What if he does? what Then!

## m of <u>M</u>ore Matinee Man

i Want more "s"—to be curled like an "s" in his breath, over his legs, under his arms. To be through his groin around the neck. I'd like to be "Ess-sening" *within* his dreams. But that's not all—or enough, I ex-pect my limbs to reach to his noises and shades, I anticipate for-matting my territories into "E," a walk on the wild side. Desire within common alphabets. And then, would he, could he? after the roller coaster, after the ferris wheel, after the merry-go-round, would he be so kind as to offer to complete my curiosity in "x"? **And not just "x"—** Kawabata, and plots, kisses, and religion; gardening, his lovely torn jeans jacket and who pays the bills which translates to mean "his wife": how will she be honored? Then, we canplay hide and seek.
**But first, he must call.** Or, I must E-Mail or fax or send my drama into his hands which type like mine. His fingers which turn pages of lousy and great books like mine. i will send him my love on the page and how could he resist a poet, an essayist, who by the nature of the genre—Creative Non-fiction—be merely re-coding facts.

I hope he smiles when he reads our—my response to his sweet body.
**Honestly,** I don't know if sex would be as great as how I wrote it, but I do know Norm and I like to talk. We like the small adventures that don't damage or interfere with our routines, probably because we write art grants—worst, literary art grants—and know how to match and stretch a budget. I love you Norm, you brilliant unknown literary adventurer.

**Now i will describe his kiss: equally textured as his voice.** The kind of kiss lily pond likes to read about, the kind humans only dream of feeling. It was longlasting, an epic. God, I love his pale hair and pale face and teeth and everything else connected to his Vikingness. And as soon as my eyes see images upon waking, his white pleasure: there. Here.

**NORM, can we be in a ka-wa-ba-ta movie next time?** but can I write it instead? And can I be smiling when you leave on the train while it's snowing?
Can there be more shots of us smilingMore than plotting *how* we could be smiling more?
And could i wear my short black skirt with my new black heels with the T-strap across the ankle while i hang on you at some literary scene?
Could we let *les autres* Imagine we are having both *angst* and climaxx at the same time?

Will you press ooyourr literarylips onto mine and whet my appetite so I can interpret us in Chinese? Filipino? Arabic? Tahitian? CNN? black and white ideographs and *hula*?
mr. norm, whats the possibility of us crushingour syntaxes while behaving like honor roll students?
Can we employ each other?
**Nor/man, wll you talk dirty 2 me on the telephone?**
please spend the night sometime so we can find out—you know—i dont know (we'll find out something), cudja?

of course, you know I'm just practicing English. But hold me longer next time Norm No.
Love me longer. Feel it freer next time.
Close your eyes a little
**close your brain a little more**.
a-litle

## LA DIFFERENCE ENTRE HIER SOIR ET NOUS

ERROR IN TRANSLATION?
Lastnight, yesterday: lastnight lasting inside my very delicate and small nipple which he so sucked like ginger pulling poooling, polling all my attention to my little spot below my *piko* which accidently and then later not so accidentally, he tried: to invade. As soon as he discovered that there existed an element not yet named in his universe, he required exploration. I guess I have to xerox the

meaning of *piko* from *Nānā I Ke Kumu* (Look to the Source). Of course, he may not *nānā* after all in which case all the *'aumākua* in my short and weak body would have to send a biblical message to Norm that would leave him short-circuited for the rest of his painful days on earth into worst thereafter where there are no rules.

*That* **said: I love his stranger in the night.** So much that I am now between the lines of *Trilogy*.

> but if you do not understand what words say
>
> how can you expect to pass judgement
> on what words conceal?

These words by H.D.—every mother every aunt or female friend should sing to herself.
Sing it like a personal and collective anthem.
Girls, remember this tune. It protects your sacred life. While most formal education and books are an evil to the spirit and voice of a young girl, these lines I found in a book. These lines have traveled with me through marathons of argument and still they lie beside the tub or dusty near the night stand. I gave each daughter a copy of these words but unless they chose to find them, this powerful song can only be heard by me.
If anything should, might, could be remembered by my fingers urgent to clear the muck so I could smell the tree bark or flowers, or see *something*, remember the words by H.D.
Alas, the world is such become a junkyard.

WITH THAT SAID, What middle-aged woman wouldn't want to have lived yesterday and lastnight? First it was Heman, the friendly and reasonably attractive Frito Lay guy who is going to be taking me out for coffee or *something*. He is part of my slightly-older-than-me-guy-dilemma—like pudding or putty? I like that. Down to earth—so far—I like that too.—maybe I won't like that later. Mr. Free—toe is the first Chinese American who has asked me out on a date (on the continent). The guys in Hawai'i don't count. It's like they were more Chinese upper middle class than American.

Later, the man who used to be married to me came and made his monthly payment to me—which I didn't anticipate because earlier yesterday he had mentioned that he would come only if his schedule allowed. Well, when he arrived, "I was about to masturbate. Come on in," and was interrupted (you know how *that* is). Steve was here to talk about the kitchen remodeling and/but/or was tired and I was too so we agreed to take a nap because it was so hot. As *xiansheng* showered, I decided to shower tooo—after all, I did get sweaty as I prepared to Be sweating (when I was going to masturbate). I din't consider Steve considering his own sexual urges which could be delivered by la waitress with no clothing on sitting beside him as we both watched the Dodgers-Cincinnati playoffs. And in between me weeping "Nomo, Nomo" he asked if I wanted to fuck. At my age, never knowing when the next one would avail itself, I reasoned "Waste not, want not."

**Of course he was a jerk after it was all over** as has been his routine lately. Thank god Norm called and came over in the heat of the dark and warm October evening. I had a *ki* leaf wrapped around my neck and foot because my foot has been hurting and there's some gahla-gahla (not gala gala) in my throat. Norm imagined that I had on a sweatshirt and knitted scarf around my neck because I was afraid he might get sexual with me.
"Mais non!" I said, "Can't you smell the Vicks?"
Norm dived straight for my chest or breast, my lungs, the nipple.
"I love Vicks," he promoted as his head went into my neck and slipped in my inner ear.
His powerful Nazi wrists and beautiful long fingers fixed my forearms as necessary. N: o(r)Ma, I love him. Oh, the part about sex that is so good! His fingers (separate what we can feel in [isolation, independent] sovereignty is what I call it) His fingers "manipulate."
And then he would say
"Do you feel that breeze?" which arrived and escaped so uneventfully. Definitely Toyoda, Bergman, and who is the guy that did "Remember My Name" with Geraldine Chapman and Anthony Perkins? There is a great song called "The Love I Have for You," sung by an unforgettable Alberta Hunter. **Never forget that movie**—the bestest.

### MYSEXUALHISTORYINREFERENCE TO AEROBICFOREPLAY

**Well, I was so excited,** naturally, I became frightened what with this **month's Vanity Fair** directing me to be in touch with my true self—
the lost little baby vegetable *real* me—

the one who usually feels like *Bu Yau Shu Cai*
—remember that name? Unwanted Vegetables.
Now I know, it was an error in translation: what I *meant* was Lost Little Baby
Vegetables. And feeling like a baby, I revealed my inner-most baby: I showed
Norman the cotton that I sleep with—the faithful cotton that remained with
me from childhood to now. To be replaced when lost or too small. I know he
thought it was kinky, but with that introduced, I searched for my Babar tapes.
I tested him too: what was the name of Babar's girlfriend and wife? Norm *ne
connait pas. C'est Celeste c'est entendu.* He couldn't remember Cornelius either.
*C'est dommage.* I couldn't find Babar so we listened to *Le Petit Prince en anglais*
which was cheerful, then Norm—or Jean, which is what he likes to be called
when we speak french to each other—
this went on and on: between my legs, whether he kissed or pumped, he was
like a Preferred Gold Card. **Nobody** is allowed to get this close to me.

I require potential suitors to select readings from my Publication List—from
all genres—and if they are **earnest** in flattering me, naturally they Should be
able to quote me frequently. How else could I be guaranteed that the trolls
understand something about me? I suppose if they want my slave act, they
shall write something "timeless," "universal" of epic literary insight about me or
donate millions of dollars to my nonprofit or do something worthwhile. Women
do it all the time. After all, it is clear that animal sex is what most males are
concerned about and just not to confuse me with Thanksgiving and the stuffing
between the turkey; needy as I am, this form of "Application" is *de rigueur.*

The writer Virginia Tom said, "Man, Carolyn, you are narcissistic!" and for a
moment he had me believing but I promptly corrected, "No, I'm insecure."

*Jean dit: embrasser moi.*
*Alors*
**C'est aujourdhui vendredi le quinze octobre mille neuf dix-neuf cinq**
ah


## DEmain

One man left his tie on the chair and
milk inside which I watch stream out as I pee.
*L'autre* wrote poems on my body and left

beer in the bottle near the bedroom door.
In the world of men, sperm is what counts:
but whose world is *This*?

On the days thereafter, there is the tie. There is the bottle.
During the night when both were here
the fence, rotted: fell over.

I love living alone.
I love not having to argue with someone in the morning.
The ripeness of fruit lasts so briefly.

Sure I'd like to have a man hold and kiss me in the morning
and if I rent the right movie, I can be She
woman eternally happy struck by the pause button
in the remote control. She has no thoughts.
She is a statement in black and white.
She is acting, her job.

Real woman is feeling her breast for patches of ruin.
This woman is not ideal:
why is the (fe) and (wo) rooted in "him"?

Some days she will not cook because the sun's light upon the tree across the
street
is sweet and common like herself and
she need not analyze this but
simply look or dream or stare or believe
breathing
long as she is.

## Back to Norm/, (et) al

Finally, his face. *Fin:* the end of waiting and dreaming was over (temporarily).
He was standing in the foyer. He didn't look spectacular but it was because he
was scared, which he didn't say until *it* was all but over (so he said).

**"It" c'est nos routine**. *It* is our mouth dance: the stuff we always do. I mean I didn't plan to have a kind of a lunch ready. I was so afraid that since Billy died and I was so worried about my baby sweetheart Billy's partner, mon *especiale* Thomas, that I couldn't really do two weeks' work within two days—and it was catching up.

So I worked ths mrning AND, I wanted to look spec Tac ular.

It was hard concentrating but (heh, heh) I pulled it off. The lunch part wasn't so dramatic. I made him comfortable by not talking about *US*. I filled in the space with prattle. I turned the kitchen into a zendo and we may as well have been meditating on our beloved navels. We may as well have been discussing a solution to the Peace Plan for Bosnia. And any time I looked at him, he was nervous that I was going to ask

"When are you going to fuck me?" or

"Well, is your body still feeling the excitement *id* had for me? or

**"Please press the 'start' button"**

One minute, he's Mr. Matinee Idol; the next he's Mr. Mop Closet. One moment, his tongue had transported my clit into unheralded lust; the next he's Normal Excuses. When he tells me he has read seven books on his vacation with his wife to Baja, you gotta know, I wondered about all that reading. Oh, and he did sleep: apparently, he slept a lot. Some WASP relationship he's in. No wonder he was "reluctant" to say much but later admitted "I'm kinda concerned about getting sucked in."

"Sucked in?" I'm thinking but say, "I want you to be *sucked in*."

I'm seeing that as long as it is I—the woman—that is being the sucker of someone's "inner-ness," then it is perfectly fine to be under the spell of the Moody Cock, but if it is a matter of a reversal—Monsieur Perfectment initiating the physical aspect—then it is legal, *de rigueur*, "accepted behavior," and after (Ab)Norm baited me into his kingdom of restraint, he Believes    he can get away with this shit from me Who is still beautiful, speaker of many languages, a good fuck and    above all a Poor Loser?

Now I'm into Plan B, the Chinese Ice Princess mode. That liar Jason said

"I promise you, he'll call."

Well, when Norm calls, I'll just have to be "hurt," "rejected"; "unattractive" is a good operating word. Then I'll say, "I thought my account had been 'cancelled.' " If I really want to fuck with his head, I'll beg for forgiveness. **And ordinarymale that he is will be** PUZZLED. I'll act like I'm so so Ashamed of what I did to turn up the drama. **In his good English, he'll be** "bewildered," and in my best Japanese servant self, I'll make like "Beat me now." Finally, I'll reveal how after days of crying and urged by all my friends, I was "healed" by recounting the story of my ill-fated no-love affair with Norm by being bribed to "share" his identity with the lit community.

Let He-Who-Refused-To-Fuck *Ono Ono* Girl swim in that moment of enjoying the notoriety
while trembling with the sobering reality that his name could be Humpty Dumpty on the NET.

Or, I'll just hand him pages 125–38 of the text and watch him contract.

Kathleen said that when she comes to visit, we can call Norm up on the telephone.
Ooowheee . . . I can hardly wait.
**Long live King Kahuka!** (a gift from the lovely and famous novelist Kathleen A)

## La Caroline N'est Pas Exactment Jeanne Moreau

Who can ever remember the names of the woman in "The Summer House," "The Bride Who Wore Black," "Jules et Jim," and "Elevator to the Gallows"?
We remember that pouting mouth.
The car cruising over the bridge into the water.
All the cigarettes and bottles of wine and kisses under and outside of the sheets.
That would be Jeanne Moreau. When I saw "Jules et Jim" again the other night, I realized I lived my life based on Truffaut's muse.

Unlike my now ex-husband who due to frustration, stupidity, or plain bad manners—broke dishes; stabbed a knife into a door; threw an iron at me (and later claimed that he didn't aim to hit me! so therefore, it couldn't constitute *really* throwing an iron at me—how philosophic)—I broke wine glasses, threw my first husband's digital clock radio out the window; and everyone else but me can remember all the "destruction" I committed in my life—not for attention, not for revenge, not to be abusive: I was living up to my Jeanne Moreau ideal constructed in the sixties by Truffaut.
I mean what guy wasn't drooling over Moreau and what chick wasn't overworking her psyche to be the local Jeanne?
My friend, the writer Faye Kicknosway now Morgan Blair IS Jeanne Moreau en Hawai'i—go visit her: Morgan is doing *Jeanne en vacances en travaillé dans l'université.*

At forty-nine, now I get it. I'm over her. Though what intrigues me more is that both Moreau and my other favorite Gena Rowlands never played Jane Fonda in real life and went in for the plump and no cosmetic surgery. However, I am a little concerned about Jeanne with so much red in her "empress" years. She kinda looks like a corvette. The cigarettes have killed her voice because you can barely hear the lines though you are compelled to watch her on the screen.

Plain talk, Rowlands who is another "Lip Master" is aging gracefully. In any of the Cassavetes close-ups, watch the lips. Not only is she delivering a message, she is *delivering*. God! she is stunning and that's another smoker. It really makes me want to go out and buy a pack of Lucky Strikes or Gauloises. Catherine Deneuve—bless her icy heart—lets her t-*res jolie* body get into some *difficulte, mais pas comme* Jeanne et Gena.
Which brings me back to Norm and me realizing that I was honed on black-and-white movies, predominately black-and-white foreign flicks.
Bien sure, I'm gonna expect more from a guy than
what James Bond or what Fabio would deliver.
I Expect some sentences.
And would it be too much to anticipate some serious wacky behavior?
I hate Chinese movies because they are too damn sad. Nothing weird about the individuals making their own demented choices. Like you could never have "Le Bon heur" as a Chinese film. Nobody chooses lust when you gotta bend your back and go into the rice paddies with leeches the next day. I love the French. They honestly believe that they are all gay paree And they are so existentially insistent on being l'example of culture.
Poor fools, it's only because the nasal way they talk leads them to believe that they are a brainy folk.
*Eh bien*, food is only a distraction in their culture: when they're not cooking or eating, they are wearing these *tres gauche* bows and rouge—*les costumes* from the era of Tante Marie Antoinette *et tous les mondes savons quoi* happened to her exceptionnne Les Francais.

As you can see—*vraiment*—I was raised by French nuns from the time I was five until I was eighteen and then Goddard and Truffaut took over. During that period, I had an affair with Goethe and Rilke. I had a string of affairs with *les autres hommes* from *Allemagne*. Christ, German men are rough. They are so butt- and teeth-bound, their bodies operate like their famous car engines or othodontics.
Which brings me back to Norm. I am so turned on to Norm because

unlike the attorney who said "No I'm not going to take you out anymore.
I try too hard with you,"
and I *had* to say, "*Maybe* I'm not worth it";
unlike that bald short and fat Chinese maestro who upon leaving me lectued
"When I get married, I'm type to stay home every night because I that kind of
man.
Not you, when you get married, you goin out.
You *too* social."
—unlike these jerks, married Norm doesn't scold me for not being more leaning
to him;
and therefore, I lhohnnggg to be with Norm.

**What a great movie**


## Grown up Response Efforttss<sub>sssss</sub>$$$$

**One day I'm feeling somewhat secure and that fuck Bryan calls. He's not
normal of course.** When he calls the second time, he knows I will be home
because he calls at 11:56 pm. I am asleep and awake—Bryan's favorite state for
me.
Don't knee-jerk the interpretation: I love Bryan.
BuTTt, He is always putting me to a test to see if I still love him no matter what.
He's
married and we don't have a physically sexual thing happening but
everything happens "between" "inside of" us: w{e} came from the same breath.
So I tell him the latest about Norm and he tells me
      "Do**n't** get emotionally involved with this guy"
which wakes me up because I A&M "inlove" with this guy.
Bryan knows I'm unstable because Bryan is unstable and Bryan
is eEEEmotionally involved with me. No matter what *les hommes parlent*
all the ones who get involved with me—it's Always emotional,
my weakest strength because I cannot distinguish my emotion from my brain
And have no interest in separating the two from my *mane'o*, the impulses
in my groin.
      "He's NOT going to LEAve his **wife**.
      —Do you talk about his wife?"
"Well, he did *mention* that he was not going to leave her."

"I mean, I'm sure he must like you more than just the physical stuff but
he   l o v es his wife:
it's his comfort zone."

Then
I was Really    AWAKE.
The fire department was on its way.

Bryan philosophized, "It's fuck'n amazing.
You're going to be fifty.
You know everyt**h**ing there is to know about the multicultural shit
you ar fuck-n brrillllnnnt AND
# you don't have a handle on the man thing.
And I don't have a handle on the woman thing either."

(This [Bryan, et al.] is: the kind I am **CLOSE** to—boy does truth hurt)

Then he sez, knowing he has gone way overboard as he stands at a pay phone
in the Tenderloin,
        "Some weather we've been having, huh?"

Weather? Now I really want to kill him but today as I write this, *c'est un autre
jour. A l'apres midi*, by mid-afternoon while I am crying because I am missing my
sister and father as I listen to Keali'i Reichel sing *"Kawaipunahele"* it is misting
outside; Thomas phones.

To all my close friends, I tell them everything—I don't know if the men Can
and DO tell me everything—but at the moment, I am really missing my sister.

        •Brrinng, brinnng *ou* celllulaa, lar; or eh-leck—tron-neek!•
*Ah oui, c'est mon* childhood *chou chou qui* calls from New York. —*Pas aujoud'hui*,
I don't entertain him today but tell him Everything including that I am in love
with a married man.
        Craig b-l-o-ws up.
        "He's: M-A-R-R-I-E-D!!!"
I'm jealous (to the point)
        You know this guy for eight years!

Eight years! (his voice raises)
    As long as you've been married?
You've known me since we were sixteen!!!!!!!???
       (ah now, the banker is calculating)
You can *talk* to him! You can TALK to him!
      What do you do with me???!
**I identify and GIVE (aka FREE) you *the* best legal and financial direction**
**And.** your family doesn't listen
**I**   **Continue to advise you**   on your finances.
AND you never pay attention to what I say.

**I** am here
your personal reassurance.
**Why** don't you have some fun with **ME!**
—Did you get that job at the UH?

I'm coming through San Francisco during the first week of the new year:
you want to be with a MarriedMan? be with a marriedman with Money and
Power: And YOU—I bet that's not enough to entice you but how about?

# MarriedMan:Money:Power
# Same Lastname as Carolyn

*come to Singapore and Hong Kong with me: it'll be great this time of year"*
                            *les bons mots* (The magic words)
although I know it is monsoon weather.
—I could bring my suits and glasses and look like his translator.

**What shall *Ono Ono* Girl**
**dOOOOOOOOOOOOOOOO$$$$$$$$$oooo?**
                                   e-mail: OOG@imua.hawaii

a) Ask her local married boyfriend for advice?

b) Write her ex=husband (whom she loves) for advice since he will not talk to her?

c) Consider options in terms of material for book

d) Call Spottie Dottie; if the line is busy fax, Hello Kitty

e) **Other**

*Kōkua*: **Write in your response and Help *Ono Ono* Girl make a good choice. Choose as many as you like or create a new Choice.**

*Mahalo*

—ghhd, hand me an orgasm

## *THE* Pivotal Question

WHo **loves me?**
I purposely did not particularize the question as to "open the field" as it were; to indicate equaminity (*mon concept favorite*); and to force the burning question in all of us.

**How? was I so bold to ask the question?**
It began with Mr. Braces (whom I have never met), a senior civil engineer who apparently will be "taking time off to do some soul-searching"—why so late??? Does a bridge have to collapse before it dawns on the Primary Force that maybe, maybe . . .

Then there's my mother who is a pest to my creative freedom. Oh she's a good provider which is how or *maybe* why she liked that I had husbands and the pressure was off (in her mind) when I simply wasn't "seeking orgasm." While she is a saint to everyone but me, she would rather play tough than let her heart spill its life with mine. Maybe she's been a vertical column so long that it is impossible to convince her that she would like me. She could almost have fun with me. Maybe it is because she lives thousands of miles away and that my relatives are so uptight that in order to preserve her good name, she has to be an in-life statue—come to think of it, my father was a statue too. As for me, I have no desire to ever be a statue—or even be remembered. I have no long-term goals; only immediate, and by now any *lōlō* should know what they are: if no, go back to Introduction. Anyway, for a while, Mildred was saying

　"I just want to be loved" along with
"I like my tea light and my men dark."
　"I get along with everybody."
"Who wants to eat pork chops all the time?"
When Ana was creating "filler conversation" and asked Grandma what she was going to wear to the Chinese New Year's dinner, Mildred *shuo*
"I'm going to wear a G-string and be the belle of the ball."
　—that jolted the granddaughter into Consciousness
So while my mother pretends that Nothing Affects Her at Her AGE, she does whatever she can to get attention.

**We all want to be loved because collectively we (possibly even Bill Gates) know(s) there is only Nominalism on which we can depend—the word or concept that is supposed to stand for something but—my kids' father's favorite term—there is no guarantee that concept exists.** What to do but to give take, steal, borrow (as in adopt or kidnap); stare at the television while Oprah manufactures and re-invents Love on a grand scale. So I asked some folks who had been, might still be, or were in fact still "in love" or at least could still feel "some" or "a lot of" love for yours truly. Of course I "surveyed" the men informally and I have to ask my publisher, attorney, 'aumākua, Kasumi, and Bryan if I should tell you the results or include it in my next book because . . .

And as this screeches to a halt, I believe that I will say a little something about loving one's own image and likeness through the example of Kasumi, "Hello Kitty," my friend, a contender for being one of Japan's first astronauts.

# 5

# *ONO ONO* GIRL'S *Hula*

## *ONO ONO* GIRL'S *Hula* (aka Introduction)

This is about the sacred and sweet: nobody "in their right mind" will talk about this but I'll try. This is about intimacy: About animals in the trees—like Daphne or big and older folks who still like to play in mud. This is something beyond English which cannot Truly be understood in English. If owls and sharks could tell this story in words, then these are the words they would translate their lives into. This is the real: no right, no wrong. Only feelings, good feelings. Here male and female mate. Other varieties come after. First there is Papa and Wākea, *wahine* and *kane*. First, there is the pretty and strong complex aroma. Who is this? *li hing mui, kahili* ginger, *lau lau* singing, "Time to eat."

**My mouth licks owl's genitals while owl shrieks longing for me who cannot be human.**

**Crying, I beg shark to chew me hard. Dig . . . dig me deep.**

**Help yourself to my bloodline. Pull and knot the cords freely.**

**Tattoo your thrust in the small of my spine.**

**Protect my sacred ears which lengthen from my heart to brain.**

**Stay until you can: linger no longer** in this ordinary tradition, in which calmly, we are alive briefly.

*Ono* Girl's Song poorly, poorly translates into English. With the exception of

Hawaiian, her natural body, other languages are not sufficient. To know *Ono* Girl, to really know *Ono* Girl, one must struggle with her shy and often frightening dance. Among her family—her *hānai 'ohana*, the family who adopted her, she is named *Ono Ono* Girl because of her lovely body which creates comfort in everyone to be so delighted and relaxed: happy to "share in her great enthusiasm for living." *Ono* Girl invites you to eat life. Eat love, eat more, fall asleep in love waking up to live, fall down, fall down again, deep.

Cry hard and pick up, dance and dance singing, laugh and laugh dancing. Go ahead, have a good cry. Isn't the song, life is such beauty? *Nani*, so so *nani*

## Five Thirty Hawaiian Time; Eight Thirty Somewhere Else

This is weird. Today is the second day at home and, as usual, I can't figure out who I am and how old I am? Yesterday, I was among the eighty-year-old Long's Drugstore Vetrans followed by the Fook Yuen Sunday Brunch crowd. As usual, every day that I'm here, I'll be eating like it is always my first meal and my first good meal in a long time. When I mentioned this to Aunty Mabel—you remember her?—she kindly reminded me of the Maryknoll days when "you looked like a basketball." Nonetheless, having left the soupy grayness of cold; collectively shared personal angst; the art biz scene; the Giants in combat; my kid about to bunt for college; my in and out husband; the Hawaiians and our evolutionary jokes, I find myself *here*, the other zone, the notquite, the fiftieth state but not really, international but American: it's a vacation to most people but it's home—that is HOME, hOme, hoME—for the rest of us, the plantation and cannery workers; the *maka'āinana*, siblings and descendants of the slop man, *lei* ladies, missionaries now not so well respected but still feared; still the best to all who left for better or worst.

Today, ma and I did our regular Long's Drugs ritual, which we do within the first forty-eight hours of my arrival. This done, in tandem with my eating of *Gau Chee Mien* at the Golden Eagle Restaurant, I am free to then proceed to visiting aunties, cousins, and maybe a bit of self-discovery! Whee, freedom.

What did I do today? I found myself impulsively walking two blocks from my mother's house to the Varsity Theater, which I have been dying to do for years. The heat sent me today. Man, this is hot weather. How do people *work* in this weather? And how do they study? Don't kid yourself: if you make it through the University of Hawai'i, you should really pat yourself on the back—except of course—if you get your degree in tourism, which is a free ride and all the coupons you can get. Gotta tell you something—am I kidding myself to imagine that I could return home to think and *work* in this weather? I could faint in this weather. I could sleep in this weather. I am already attuned to shopping for brief periods of time at *Ala Moana* in this weather. Boy, folks like to eat and shop and shop and eat here—even at Summer Session I heard a guy treat the subject of "refried beans on special at Safeway, nonfat," but he was behind a cubicle so I couldn't see him. He did mention chips too, and almond rocca. Man, people are always talking and dreaming food and shopping. Eh, I can get into fights very easily in this weather: the trick is in the breathing. Just breathe and walk to the bathroom, look out at the enticing *ti/ki* leaves, the palms shaking their 'ōkole, the bluest sky in the world, and return like a god.

I can eat this weather. The *pakalana*, white ginger, *pīkake*, and stephanotis at my mother's house hypnotize any rational senses. I hate the idea of air conditioning—breathing recycled dust particles day in and out—but work in this natural weather, I don't know. How about all the people who jog, play tennis, drive in stop-and-go butt to butt, walk-with-the-umbrella, or wait-for-the-bus in the sun in this weather? Maybe if I was located at another spot with breeze and surf lying in and out mixing with just the right amount of sand, maybe if there was Hawaiian music and a black-and-white silent movie featured before my eyes, then maybe the story would be different, but meanwhile while the heat influences my body and psyche, I gotta adjust to it.
Da end. Whoa da moss.

On the way to Varsity Theater, I passed my childhood. The Marciels who played music all the time and smooched under the green orange tree and hugged and called each other "dahling." He played the bass and she, the piano, to the beast of a sa-lid, I mean solid one-two, one two three beat, and they sang like love birds nectar in their eyes and throats—their romantic house followed by Mrs. Aguiar, who worked for Liberty House, and always showed us the gorgeous red dress that she intended to be buried in. When I was a kid and used to walk past her house with those red kind of bushes, I used to always hope that she would get her wish. Now that those bushes have been replaced with a chain-link fence, you realize that dreams and symbols change, but you can't get too deep into this kind of thing in Hawai'i, not in this heat, not when the overt manifestations *appear* like tradition—especially the First Day.

Maybe it's those *haole* magazines that give me theese kind ideas; maybe anybody can see this if you take a heat break.

The Zanes now live in the Marciel house. Mr. Zane is always polishing his car and willing to practice my Mandarin with me. Lately, my mother has been scolding me about not being able to understand my Hakka because of a strong *guo yu* accent.

One day Mrs. Zane was visiting and my mother was yakking to somebody on the telephone. That was the perfect opportunity for me and Mrs. Zane to speak both Hakka and *guo yu*. As I swiched, she followed. Mrs. Zane can speak several dialects of Hakka as well as many dialects of Mandarin. As we were talking stories, I asked Mrs. Zane if she could understand me when I spoke Hakka to her.

"I understand you Perfectly," she exclaimed sm(hi)iiling,

which could only make me wonder what my mother is really saying to me.

Later, over cigarettes and beer on a warm and rainy 4th of July, their lovely daughter Dottie and I laughed about our families as I started the coals for the barbeque that me and ma would always remember. It was so great sitting under the carport, our backs to the street as we wondered if the bananas were ripe enough to be picked.

Then the very Best happened: ma and I ate the potato salad and seaweed and short ribs while we watched white people on television celebrating the holiday in DC. Why were We watching white people watch somebody entertain them? It definitely was an audience of white folks with no Marion Barry around. Eventually though, I remembered that I had purchased these sparklers which I had hoped would return a feeling from my childhood. NOPE. They were duds, but as I was outside in the warm dark, the memory of the fig tree behind me, *pakalana* strongly chanting near plumeria flashing its hot scent into the stillness, I saw a rainbow in the night and ran inside to grab ma by the elbow. Poor ma. So much excitement! and romantic in the backyard among the *ti* leaves and avocado tree.

man oh Man, I wanted to cry I was so happy! I held that bone and skin next to me loving Loving my mother in a way that I was unprepared for. We leaned against each other to watch the silent worlds of Blake and Confucius, Walt Disney, and our ancestors spring and flood our eyes with neon zeal. Of course, we joked: it was so intense. So mother-daughter. The measurement of time beneath the arches of our feet tasting so so *ono*.

Here I must cross the street for a sentence or two. Mrs. Eaton would be surprised if I don't mention her especially since we are now cousins through the Crowinburgs. Especially since her eighty-seven-year-old cousin Joe is the current flame of me and Annette—bless his heart—but beware of how my family uses the terms "sweetheart," "lover," "boyfriend": we don't care. It's just to kiss up to that insecure male ego—EXcept for Mr. Kumalae (so cute in his bermuda shorts), whose daddy made *ukulele*. Hakka girls say whatever we please leaving smoke or dust or heaven while our big gorgeous feet speed away.

Beyond Mrs. Aguiar house live Mr. and Mrs. Kumalae, who are the real *ali'i* of the neighborhood. Mrs. Kumalae, a Hakka girl from School Street, is ninety and she looks young! And she is bright and super together. What is her secret? maybe her Hawaiian husband, her daily walk, and picking ma's white ginger. She picks ginger everyday "to make the flowers come out more." And now, she's picking *pakalana*—those so small hard to pick easy to bruise so so good to smell *pakalana*. And you wanna know what for? for me! She picks enough *pakalana* until she has enough to make me a three-strand *lei*. Can you believe it! Nobody does this kind of stuff on the mainland. Nobody's gonna take the time to be so nice. This could only happen in Hawai'i.

My mother's boyfriend Mr. Pang lives across from the Kumulae's. Ma actually hates Mr. Pang but she started a habit a long time ago by calling the Egg Man, the Laundry Man, the Gas Station Man—any guy who was sweet with her was her "boyfriend." Mr. Pang only lacks a number in the long line of Mildred's boyfriends. Now but, ma got young REcycle boy-Man. He, tall. He, cute. He say, "Aunty, I hang clothes for you."

The other night we were sitting in the livingroom which everyone in the world can look through because we have louvers and it is so hot that they have to be open because we are natural air purists. You get used to it after years of humiliation and self-consciousness. Anyway, we were sitting there oppressed by the heat and *ayecudiyou*! I jump up in the power-ranger stance and with my two arms and hands extended as machine guns point out my mother's latest and most god-like boyfriend, the *mo'o*. Who is *mo'o*? a gecko or common lizard to most of the world. But to HERE, any uncontrollable anything is deemed vicious and worthy of death. My mother's heart leaped for the spray. I said, "Forget it.

You won't see it soon enough." Oh, Mildred was agitated, she wanted that *moʻo* dead. It just reminded her of when daddy was alive and she used to get after him to kill the *moʻo*, but when he couldn't, she proudly "wouldn't speak to him for days." My mother, Miss Perfect, wouldn't speak to my father because he couldn't—maybe *wouldn't*—kill a lizard!

After the Mesicks' house, I don't know too many houses except for Elmo Wong's—the tall cigar man who had those beautiful rainbow plumerias in his yard. Now, there are new houses with new plants. There is actually some lively and lovely style with the house that has squash and beans languishing in its front yard next to its relative cement structure with fertile *boo look* and green grass. Talk about green grass, the only green grass on the street is owned by these folks and the Japanese Chamber of Commerce, that has the most imposing structure on the street nearer to the University side. It was already Big, but it had to resurrect to become bigger. So, my little street goes commercialand I don't know just how much I hate that new structure because I read that there's a gallery there now . . . maybe if it continues to be so upscale, I could walk down the street, drink a *skoosh* bit of *sake* and *bonzai, pal mal merci.*

This is what I was inhaling on the way to the Varsity, which during the Sixties I had heard had become a lecture hall! My baby memory of a theater where I walked to on the weekends with a dime in my hands. Sometimes, I ran barefeet with only that dime between my fingers. I can't remember how many black-and-white matinees were like vitamins to me. Me and the usually empty theater like it was today for this uneventful foreign film called "White." Sometimes I got jujubes stuck in my teeth. Once, at the water fountain, I even saw my older sister at the same movie that I was at!
That movie theater means something to me.
If I try real hard, maybe I can remember going to the movies with my mother at night, a real excitement because then we would always race home against the thought of burglars or rapists or who-know-whats.
Now we walk to the bank, which is next door to the theater, or the other bank, which is across the street—the banks that you can not wear dark glasses or a hat into because of all the robberies. For real, **can not**.

Thank god, the Varsity is still there at five dollars and ninety cents heavier. The soda fountain across the street *hele* on to somewhere else and so did this *keike.* *Pau hana*

## *An Den*

By ten o'clock in the morning, it is too hot. Seven o'clock at night or morning, too hot already. Whoh man. On the way from my mother's house (it used to be my parents' house until my daddy went to be with the *'ohana 'aumākua*), some of the sounds remind me of China. The constant pounding, rat-tat-tatting; the whizz of some fanning-like drill from the dentist's office; but more monsterish is the old guy who yesterday was repainting the blue utility pipe who today is sitting on a wooden stool and shaving the grass by hand. By hand! cut-ting the damn grass by hand! what? the Japanese Chamber of Commerce can not give the guy one hand lawn mowa? Gotta have so much art. I can't decide if I'm jealous, in love or am diss-gusted with the Japanese: art in the food; art with tea; art when you give a gift; always so neat—the old man was very artful—by hand!

It is so darn hot
soo Hot so so hohTT
(becuss we are so sSensitiff, ov coss)
—summertime, middle of the afternoon by Bay area standards and the colors in the shower blossoms, the ordinary red hibiscus, the clutches and bunches of aloe plants which everyone has incase of an emergency which never happens while the aloe continues to regenerate—the swampiness of birthing is blinding.

The shower trees which the elder cousins and aunties hate because of the dead shower blossoms that they have to rake to keep the yard looking so green and soft and nice. Man, those shower blossoms possessed me to imagine that I was a young pretty bride season after season. Even as an old fut I still feel so excited to see those cumulus happenings of yellow and buff and rouge and passion-fruit orange, rainbow pink, and lemonade. Blonde and shave ice strawberry, pineapple, *mai tai*, tutti-frutti, papaya, french, and lipstick deep kisses parasols tree after tree, street after street near the canals in Chinatown; along King Street infront of all those concrete buildings with air conditioners sticking out looking so ugly; where Honolulu Stadium use to be which is now a lovely park for babies to learn to walk and old folks take their daily at 5:30 am. Those showers are here to stay, tourists or not. Sovereignty or not. Who takes care of the shower trees? Aye, can learn something from the shower tree, eh!

Oh oh oh, the strong smell from the fried fast goodies and plumeria and water floating in the heat—*Au'ē*, I feel sex in around and overboard: the *ma'i lele* is

not only *kaona* but biting; and tickling my psyche and body and *imua*—
English not enough!

I am so glad that I lived in China because I can see some overlapping of China in
Oakland and now I can see some overlapping of China here, but I doubt if any
other culture can ever overlap in China because it's pretty hard to influence 1.2
billion knuckleheads. They're not good at jokes unless it is at your expense—
poor tings: that's what they're used to.

Wait a second—wait second, I heard that now, Christianity is a big thing in
China, though the Christians are getting killed. And actually, most of the Chinese
who made it to Hawai'i didnot go back to Zhong Guo. Granpa married *tūtū* and
they were happy: he never wanted no mo China. He learned to speak Hawaiian,
*'ōlelo o Hawai'i* and he never spoke Loong Doo
again. My other granpa made it to Kohala and sent for my pretty pretty granma
with the smooth sweet big feet and they fought for the rest of their lives but
they never wanted to go back to China either.
When daddy was alive, we couldn't be Hawaiian but now that it is safe to be
Hawaiian, ma teaching all these Hawaiian words which I did not know she
knew. She said *tūtū* never spoke English, always always gently spoke beautiful
Hawaiian. Was so so kind to ma. But Then, Chinese was a step up from Hawaiian
and even though daddy was half Uygur which is like Turk and Loong Doo, he
sucked in, he was Chinese except with *tūtū*. So now, my Chinese mother is
teaching me Hawaiian. Maybe someday even the Chinese can let loose when
it's safe.

**Which brings me to the secrets. A long time ago, my mother said,**
**"Nobody gives out the recipe." but me,**
**I *waha nui* big mouth, I goin essay everyting.**

For the past two days I have been reading John Charlot's work on *Kamapua'a*
and something about the politics of literature or something. Good ting that
*haole* grew up here—I went to school wit his brudder, Peter—anyway he went
write dat he got the material from here and dere and put um togeter and went
come up with dis pretty good *haole*/local resource material 'cause maybe I going
use John as a reference for my unique syntax.

Anyways, yesterday, while I *liao* with my Hakka *'ohana*, I learned something:
*Pikai!*
the rain come down!
Laughing and laughing so loud my aunties accused me of being Portuguese.
Teasing, we slice each other's breath with kung fu daggers, flips, trips, and
poetry.
Those old ladies are viciously funny and got nothing on their minds except a
good time and having the last sound.
They not so smart sometime. They not so right but they love imagining they
being right.
And they love drama.
They would never own up to it but they love staring in a down-to-earth and
up-to-Las Vegas opera. No wonder I am so goddamn dramatic. Those Hakka
women know how to put on a show, and the secret of club membership is
speaking their esoteric but very user-friendly public language. Once you can
joke in Hakka, you're in. While I don't know how to play the conventional
gambling games, I know those girls love to gamble and they love fast thinking,
an' good laugh and Action.


When you spend the afternoon at Nelia's having lunch, it is *de rigueur* to pass the
time gracefully, so you need to keep the action moving by being able to comment
quickly in Hakka and English. Your English must be taut and somewhere in
the realm of the obnoxious but your Hakka can be Rude, ssssSexual, sec-ular,
conTemptuous, Vain, VULgar, hiStoric, INdulgent. It can be incorrect and
everyone will raid the wrongdoer with fierce justice met. I mentioned some
phrases that the younger of the sisters, Aunty Alma, was unaware of, and she
was promptly educated by the two elder dowagers. Even I knew the proverbs—
though I knew them only in English. And guess what? when I began dropping
some phonemes in Hawaiian, the aunties didn't react. They were either feeling
sorry for their sister my mother or Maybe, I am coming home often enough so
that they are getting used to what a headache I was as a child and maybe in
their senior years they cannot tell the difference or bother to care. Though they
pretend not to know a lot of Hawaiian they know a lot! My Hakka grandpa loved
Hawaiian, spoke and danced Hawaiian whenever his *mane'o* kicked the *kino*.


"Of couse!" they always exclaim!
"ov cuss!"

## The Rituals

All the rituals here include eating out at the restaurants because eh! who wants to cook in this heat? By the way, I'm convinced that it wasn't this hot when I was growing up, and then we had to wear so much clothing because everything was still pretty *haole* style. Which brings me to the *haole* question: why they a'ways in management positions? You know what I mean! Everytime, everywhere they are in the top positions telling us the guidelines and the means to achieve. Look at all the contest winners in the literature: *haole.*—I wass in Cody's Bookstore—in good ole anarchist Berkeley in 1995—at a reading by two heh heh "avant-garde" white middle-aged well-preserved gentlemen. I was looking at all the photographs of the *haole* writers looking at me from the walls above. Maybe one or two big name imitation *haole* non-*haole* writers but, you know by jess looking at the wall you could tell this was a *haole* place. And the *haole* so smart, they even know how not to get what I driving at. They got all the accessories (words) to mean we not invited.

Like the message is
Come but no act like the way you act.
Act like us.
You act like us, we like you.
True, this may be the same in other countries, but this is Indian land and it would be a good idea if the logophiles would—they can but no like—remember. When non-*haole* gets something by being wannabe *haole*, we squawk, get jealous maybe but
maybe
we should "send a message"
that demonstrates in the way of my dear cousin Ah Chau Hua—Howard to the non-family members—that says

> **Just because I don't care how I dress or what I look like,**
> **I got brains and**
> **I have deep feelings for what I care about.**

Howard's a bonafide member of the local Hakka Society and knows quite a bit about the Hakka, but everyone in the family wants to avoid him because, frankly, he is not too hot looking a dude. His best friends are his dogs and birds.

Aunty Mabel, who requested not to be quoted and condemned me with a lawsuit, managed to compare Howard with a free spirit yet could not help but wonder how I saw anything in anyone who was both dull and dumb.

Aunty Alma's eyes waved to the side. She inhaled through her mouth and bit her teeth.
"Caroline, why do you want to associate with Ah Chau Faht?
You require conversation.
You require attention to detail.
I'm always on pins and needles when I have a conversation with you because you challenge folks."
My mother was giving her famous deaf-ear treatment. So when I mentioned the part about his *puka* tee shirt, everyone gasps while delighted and knows that that is his own Howard unkempt signature.

When I asked A Chau Hua if he wanted to go see a movie with me, my mother's eyeballs began to quiver. I was accused of going ToO farr.
"What?" I said,
"do you think I gave him a orgasm!"
Oh the cousins and aunties were horrified that I who used to be so intelligent was now going downhill. Now, that I'm becoming one of Howard's confidants, the family is squirming because he's dropping in more and staying longer, which forces us to expand the most simple topics to their nth degree. Then things began to get out of hand: he suggested lunch. That was out of the question, my mother bowed out as she noticed I was focusing on the hole revealing his nipple in the many-holed tee shirt that he was wearing. When I mentioned this to my other cousin who is taking me to a fancy hotel for dinner tonight—I don't know the names anymore because I am not part of the scene here—Beatrice gulped in her ever so subtle voice to remind me how busy I am and that it was really unnecessary to have lunch with Howard. After all, it's the fancy hotel tonight where I will wear my dowry of jade necklace, bracelets, and earrings; the other fancy hotel tomorrow afternoon for lunch where I will wear silk and eyeliner, hose and perfume; and more meals before they roll me onto that airplane by Tuesday.

I'll call Howard again when I come home next time. After all, he did say that you didn't have to be a guy to be enrolled in the Hakka society, and I want him to take me there in his truck. I'm sure no woman has ever been in his truck and I do like Howard. Maybe he'll even let me drive that mother—that'll give the aunties something to pout about!

## Alu Like

When I started to write, nobody in the family was aware or cared what I was doing. Then, it was exclusively poetry and nobody had the stamina to fight the heat and penetrate my own hard-headed agenda. But ever since Nelia suggested that I write fiction (which I refused to do) and I bought the computer, it's been a way of pretending that I can play the piano and prevent arthritis from its ruthless powers. When I first came home to read at the biighg university, my mother didn't know what that meant but she went along for the idea. When I read at San Francisco State University—she was visiting for my older daughter's graduation—she went to the reading because it was an outing. Now that she has read some of my work, she has a vague idea of what I do but frankly doesn't give a damn as long as I don't call her crying or tell her bad news about her granddaughters.

Now that I'm home to read with a few local writers, she mentions that "Carolyn has come home to read *at the University*." What I'm curious about is *what is understood by the person* sharing this news with my mother? because nobody asks questions—out of ignorance, saving face, or politeness. The other day after my aunts had determined that I "looked gorgeous with my new hair, and appeared like I had gained a little weight"—like I hoped they wouldn't say anything—I proceeded to be questioned by these advanced ladies of salon. Soon enough, we were discussing detailed issues of sovereignty, and eventually I gave them copies of my Cannery work. Sovereignty and the Cannery—that sounded like a bad marriage, but having talked about one or the other separately before, we talked in the familiar family way—as long as we could about one—before slipping into the other, joking intermittently.
Aunty Alma, the youngest and most advanced in the ways of the contemporary world, while high-browing the Sunday Advertiser mentioned this or that about "what the Hawaiians are doing now."

Sympathetic to their long and justified grievances, she inquired what the current state of this or that was with the Hawaiians. In Hawai'i, whenever anyone says "Hawaiians" they mean the Native Hawaiians. On the mainland or continent (depends upon who you're speaking to—if I say "continent" to my relatives, they'll think I'm being stuck-up; if I say "mainland" to "some Hawaiians," they might not like that), in California and beyond, when you say "Hawaiian," it could mean anything. A lot of non-Hawaiians consider themselves Hawaiian because of that "Hawaiian at heart" which tourism has imprinted. Aunty Alma hoped outloud. "The Hawaiians better get their stuff together, otherwise time will be running out and they won't have anything."

Did I dare challenge Aunty Alma to join the Nation, *Ka Lāhui?*
Did I dare tell her that there already is a Constitution and even some organization accomplished considering the circumstances. I played it safe, I told her about my part and how I'm interested in the *'ōlelo.* I told how her how the verbs "to be" and "to have" are not included in the language and other critical pieces like that. All the aunties are not dumb though they pretend that they don't comprehend much. They are "on medication," "too old," or any creative escape they can manage on the spot. So, when they heard this information—which made sense to them on some deep level—they did not want really to compute the expansive consequences, which is when we switched to the Cannery.

Well, I already wrote about the cannery but the aunties did not know this. My mother may or may not have read what I published about the cannery; the aunties did not until now. The discussion about the cannery began without my mother realizing up until now that Aunty Marjorie never worked at the cannery but worked at Meadow Gold dipping vanilla Milk Nickles into chocolate and she demonstrated the gesture. Before Aunty Alma even mentioned whether she had worked in the cannery or not, Aunty Marjorie had begun to read the essay I had written prior to the essay on the cannery and slowly crept on to the section where I had apparently written the words "pig's ass." And the publisher published these words "pig's ass."

"Carolyn, how come you wrote 'pig's ass'?" The introduction from my entire career of writing that my ninety-year-old aunty reads is the words "pig's ass." I guess it could have been worst, much worst I'm now even positive, but at that moment, I was hoping very hard that no one was paying attention to Aunty Marjorie. To deter the possibility of further inquiry, I mentioned that I wrote about Aunty Mabel and Bonnie in the essay and proceeded to show Aunty Alma the section. As I was hoping, she gasped with laughter and wondered aloud just what I had meant by the section describing Aunty Mabel's physical movements and mentioned

"I don't think Aunty Mabel will appreciate this description of her."

When I demonstrated the Aunty Mabel moves as portrayed in the essay, Aunty Alma instantly recognized her baby sister now in her seventies. After I rendered Aunty Mabel, Aunty Alma realized why my mother had prevented me from joining them in Las Vegas and vetoed the near possibility of me ever joining them.

"Alma, she'll invade our privacy and she'll write the naked truth about us. She won't change one wrinkle, one hair coloring, one secret. She won't even change the names," my mother snitched.

"Won't change the names!" screeched Aunty Alma as she clearly saw her sister's own name written in black on the white page.

"Alma, she wants to write about how we run around the hotel rooms in our bra and panties! You know she has no interest in gambling. The last time I went to Reno with her, she read the newspaper in the casino and wanted to go to the movies. Her husband was very uncomfortable with her behavior," reported my mother.

"What's so interesting about us?" said Alma.

"You're all so funny," I managed to suggest.

"I *never* run around the hotel in my bra and panties," corrected Aunty Marjorie. "When I went to that last trip with Nell, she and I went into the bathroom to change."

The other sisters looked into space.

Then it was time to go. It was too hot. I had just gotten off the plane.

As usual, I had made the chat complicated but I come from a mother who upon the second day when I am waking up beside her at five-thirty am asks if I want to see her hernias which are as big as two eggs.

"No," said the writer, "not so soon."

This is the same mother who walks in on my bath to ask me some questions about what the attorney said yesterday and what is the business plan for the day. This is the mother who pretends she can *not* understand too much, but present her with complex situation with finances, regulations, and ask her to respond with an intelligent insight!

She can do math the way I can do poems, and I can do a few in person for you next time.

Before we left the house ma said, "You spelled Mabel's name wrong."

*A hui hou*

# Bathing at Home

I took snapshots of the bathroom, the same bathroom that I have bathed in for the past forty-eight years. Count 'em. The same faucets, the same green color. The linoleum did not speak up and walk away, neither did the hamper. Maybe the curtains have been changed now and then and louvers installed but the essential tub, bucket, and wonder wooden stool remain ancient as history.

When I sit in the position, I relive all the long and shorter hair shampoos; the times when I was younger and my mother still washed my hair. I relive being in China and having the water turned off without notice, my long hair full of soap and me freezing in the dead of Chinese winter. Then, I shift to when I would come home and my hair was like black cotton candy and stood out perpendicular to the ground.

*Tien ah!* Did I get the Hawaiian hair when I started turning on to my Hawaiian side?

Nothing I could do controlled its own way. Now that I have really cut it to its new waves, I feel like Susan Powter, I just hope I don't behave like her. I can wash my hair as many times as I like though and I take many Potagee baths during the day.

Why are these short baths called Portuguese baths anyway?

For a long part of my life, I used to hate this bathroom because it represented something low class but now I love it. What can you do about who you really are? Why should I be like the people who continually electrocute the movie screen and magazines? I'll never be blond nor have I been to tall and back. I am the bathroom, the backyard, the venetian blinds; the dirt and sweat between my fingers.

May as well love yourself just like the music and message seems to say over and over in so many sort of ways.


# How I Met *Pono*

Today, August 5, 1994, while writing at the local Kinko's computer services, I overhear the manager say to the guy next to me that he has seen the guy's work in the newspaper before. Well, *niele* me, I gotta look, eh? So I noticed that he is doing some campaign for this guy named Morgado who is running for mayor, I think. Morgado, I thought that was an Italian name until my Aunty

Alma corrected me and told me that it was in fact Portuguese. Well, the point is that my cousin Wesley is working in the campaign for this guy Morgado so I go ahead and say,

"Excuse me, but do you know someone named Wesley Chong?"

"Wesley Chong? He's my cousin," says the young man.

I refuse to believe what I am hearing.

"Wesley Chong? No no, Wesley Chong is *my* cousin."

Now the young man and I are eyeing each other wondering who in the world we are seeing; trying to place the other with no reference whatsoever. Then, I say in that oh so *tita* voice, in that oh so old aunty suspicion,

"**What** is your **name**?"

"Pono."

"Pono? *How* are you related to Wesley?"

"Through my dad, Leonard."

"Leonard?" ("Who's Leonard?" I'm wondering. "We got no Leonards.")

"Yeh, Leonard Chong's my father."

"Leonard Chong's your father?

(**I** don't know any Leonard Chong)—and then it hits me! *How* would I know **Leonard Chong**? I have never called Leonard Chong "Leonard." I know "Leonard" as "Buggie," of course. Buggie, I know.

"Is Honsie you mother?" I ask.

"Yeah, Honsie's my mother."

"Do you know Aunty Mildred?" I ask.

"Yeah, Aunty Mildred"—and he begins to point in the direction where my mother lives about a block away.

"I'm Carolyn, Aunty Mildred's daughter."

*Now* Pono and I can not quite compute that the family is operating in the twenty-first century. Meeting a relative for the first time is a big thing. There are the rituals, the dinners. You meet your relatives at birthday parties, weddings, graduation parties, or funerals, never at the computer store—Who goes *there*? We are not a family that meets people in public places and have meaningful conversations. Pono and I cannot quite focus on our work now and we are renting at sixty-five cents a minute. We try to small-talk but can not. We cannot quite concentrate on the work, too curious about each other. That's okay, I'm almost done anyway.

When I go home and tell my mother, she can not believe it, and the family now has one more story to add to its ever-increasing list. When I told my older daughter the story she said, "Oh yeah, I think I know who he is. I never met him but I heard he was having a party the next day after Ana and I were leaving. He was having a Real party not a dinner."

Grannma does her best, she's just not twenty-four.

## Finally at the Beach

I cannot believe that I actually went to the beach today. It's been business, business businesss—my mother's of course—or eating eating eating. Today, after I went to see my daddy on the fifteenth anniversary of his death, I felt it might be safe to ask my mother if I could go to the beach.
This I did after I talked to my personal board of directors located in my psyche to remind myself that my mother just does not know how to relax. I went and bought two plate lunches—way too much food of course but she just drives me nuts telling me what I can and should buy and what I shouldn't. And god, I hate shopping with her—no browsing permitted. Anyway, after I bought the plate lunches and expected her to be anxious because I bought too much food, I mentioned casually that I'd like to go to the beach after we go to the grave. She considered.

Well, being in that tank with her is something else. She is some kind of driver. I will not drive that car, and just thinking about it gives me cramps. That car is a spaceship that has a wind-up key for an engine. Whirr-rrr-rrr, whrr whrrr whrr whrrr whrrr sings the car as it slows to a stop. Ssssueakkick go the brakes. My mother the Terminator drives that car and does some moves it in too. Like driving too close to the right-hand lane because she doesn't want to drive too close to the left lane. And she's aggressive: changes lanes fast and slow depending upon what she's up for. And she does not care for disrespect and stupidity on the part of others. Nonetheless, she drove me to Magic Island. And, I was holding my breath the whole way.

Thank god I made it to the beach. I can't believe that I lay in the sun, got wet and felt normal for a change. *Mālama pono*

## October 20 something, 1994

Crickets worrying, the sun setting in oranges, red feathers, streaks of vaudeville, and pumpkins rotting or baking in a pie. Saturday night at home without family, guy, or woman. It's really not so bad if you really want to be a writer because if what you do is write then you need the time to simply type the words out. And more work, even more, tiring, the re-write. Earlier today, I ran the narrative in my head and only because I heard the crickets, I felt compelled to write the words down. Other humans are at dinner in restaurants, maybe in line at the movies. The lucky ones are making love or about to, and then there are my buddies at the Yellow Emperor Club.

There is everything at the Yellow Emperor Club that people who browse at my neighborhood Rockridge and Elmwood street fairs do not want or are not privy to. There is every element of William Burroughs served in a contemporary Chung King platter that ain't Woman Warrior or Joy Luck Clubish—it ain't the Chinese Merican scene of the twenties, the fifties, or the eighties: it is twenty-first-century hard-core immigrant real.

Priscilla and I went there recently. We were real scared. I actually have history with the Yellow Emperor Club in that, a while back, my guy was in on the original renovation scam. Oh, he spent loads of time there imagining that he was going to become rich at last—again. He was a fucking whore for that slimy Ching and Chung now in jail or maybe marbleized on some altar. There were stories of how throngs of Chinese nearly broke the doors down waiting to apply for a job; and how the hostess and Ching had made cock and cunt contact through their eyeballs. Then, there was the gossip about the day when Ching and the so-called Eurasian hostess both walked in with wet hair. Hah! Cuntry western Californy livin on the edge in the gambling club scene. So Priscilla-and-I-nerds are the immigrants at the Yellow Emperor Club though she did look like a common gangster in all-black leather. She did drink shots of double tequila and smoke. On the otherhand, I looked like a middle-aged matron but tried my utmost to appear like the cat who ate the mouse when I saw my old buddy John Good straight from prison. A layer of stomach hanging over the belt line, greasy though recently permed hair, and bragging as usual. The very first thing he says to me is, "I heard Steve is living with his girlfriend in San Francisco." I guess I deserved that: hang with ganstas, die from them. Well, I immediately needed emergency room treatment. Cut my throat, insert the tubes. Where's the scanner? Gloves, I need gloves. Priscilla buys me another Tanqueray and tonic while she orders another tequila. We have to deal with Hoy, who references himself as Shipa Hoy in order that he can imprint artifice into our deepest psyches. With his mouthful of teeth and smoking brilliantly, he is unimpressive—as compared to the other sojourners gambling away in the suspended reality. Oh fuck, how I wish I never lusted diagramming sentences as a child! Nothing here is from the movies that I've ever seen—and I have been a devotee of the Pacific Film Archives at the museum so I have seen a lot of flicks from lotsa countries from every hour having passed on earth.

The Yellow Emperor Club is a trip though not so different from every day in and out Chinatown that the tourists and people who only come to eat in Chinatown don't wanna see. So what's it like?

What's it like? math concentration, no stare at nothing. Everybody, ev-er-rybody in there wearing black so if you go there, don't wear yellow or red unless you don't mind getting killed or losing the gold in your teeth. If you no smoke be sure you drink. Bad luck, dreams gone sour there.

## More Yellow Emperor

The other day, reluctantly, I went to a birthday party. I'm not crazy about the person but since I hadn't seen her in a safe enough long time, it was necessarily social for me to "emerge." I wouldn't go as far as saying that it was a mistake, but it was easier to be browsing at the Concord Mall with my friend Sr. Sophia. Anyway, the "birthday person" was complaining that she felt it was cruel her close friends were making a big deal that she had turned forty.

So what? I thought. She was white. Maybe she was so confused because she had adopted an African name but was nowhere close to da hood nor African cul-cha cha. She's a bored and lonely suburbanite who's been in therapy so long that when she talks to you, it's like she's talking to her therapist and she expects you to Respond favorably to that crap. *'A'ole*. No tank quew.

When you're colored and don't exist because your skin is mud, squash, sand, rock, or maybe fish, you got other things on your worry list.

So you're forty? you got all your teeth; you can walk. You got this food and wine at your house—what's the problem? Sometimes, when you got more than enough, you can not enjoy your own life. Too fuckin' bad if that's your situation. You Can suffer having too much.

Well, just as I set my feet walking to the post office to get my usual air space, I began thinking about that forty-year-old crap when dung! (or "ding" if your ears only hear English) I understand what I meant when I designed the question on that NEA Writer's Survey to ask writers if they introduced themselves as a "writer": I never introduce myself as a "writer"—bad manners in Hawaiian, but after hearing all that useless fear about being forty, I realized that I was more concerned that I'm not a real writer. Then I remembered *that* on Saturday night when I was feeling not like anyone else, and I began to write.

I realized after the fact that I may not *feel* like an anybody.
I'm no longer somebody's wife.
I don't have a job.
My kids are not around the house so I no longer feel like I'm their mother.
I definitely enjoy my relationship with my mother: we are on the same page—if you will—
And I am a writer because I don't know how to do anything else.

I also know that when you live and perceive life from three distinct cultural realities, but must always function in one, that is psychic and spiritual death—but ain't dat wha most folks do! dey gotta, because of the ever-presence of the *luna*—the white boss. How could you not be white?

Remember Skinner and his damn rats?
I am living in a house designed and built by white men.
I drive a car made by Japanese on roadways designed and operated by white men.
I eat food bought in Chinatown or Berkeley Bowl—thank my *'aumakua* for dat. Who knows where my clothes are made?
But the media, that's the big one and the publishing mileu—all that white imprinting. And Carolyn Lei-lanilau is saying almost all the time, I don't trust this shit.
An election is coming up and folks want to buy playground equipment for the schools in Oakland: why more steel in our lives? Dig up the macadam. Plant a tree. Tell the birds to *hele* on into the branches. Let there be more music not less ozone. If a kid has to fall from a tree so what? By the time the bureaucracy steals money from one pile to start another, the tree would be big. Many birds born. What's wrong with a swing hanging on a tree?
I had a tree swing. There was nothing like that swing. It would probably be the most respected item in the yard and why shouldn't it be?

The world is on a wrong course and swiftly—eagerly smacking its gutless lips on its way to no longer enjoying what we still got: this delicate sweet earth. And the people who delicately love it are already invisible; some dead, some on their way, and others like me.

I saw Evelyn (pronounced Eve-lyn) the ballet teacher yesterday. Gorgeous. Fragile because she had pneumonia and she was stunning like an *adagio*. And she reminded me of Frances, the other dancer who was with the San Francisco Forbidden City Night Club. Frances is the opposite, a show-biz tornado, grandly flamboyant. And then there's Mildred, my mother, the best, the greatest human being that I know.

What a privileged life I have!

## December 1, 1994

Home again: Well, what has happened this time since I've been back?

As I mentioned to Puhipau, I just rolled into the surf and just let myself be thrown
wherever I happen to bounce.
I didn't resist a thing.
I didn't ask any questions.
I didn't talk back—the most important.
—Even had a chance to talk about sovereignty with my cousins less than an hour after I arrived as I sat in the same house that I've sat in for what seems like a million years where I was babied and punished and loved and educated and lectured to.

It was with my favorite cousins Nelia and Beatrice, and my mother sat squeezing her legs waiting for me to humiliate her or to start a war after she had warned me Many Many times how I should never bring up "that word"—well, I didn't. The cousins just asked me what I was doing and I mentioned "education," not so much "sovereignty," and it took off. But they are smart *wahine*, my Chinese cousins, and when I told them that we no more da verb "to have" or "to be," the lights went on in their pupils—you could see that alarming neon flash like

"Oh?" or "oh!" but you knew they then knew something that they had and could never conceive = of.

Linguistics: how I love linguistics.
This is the key to me and my family. My family loves money and being right: I love being right. Meanwhile, it's too bad that being right and money do not go hand-in-hand. So I was sitting on the sofa as I have sat and as my own children have learned to sit and my Tai Yi was not there physically, but we were repeating the ritual.
We were the present-day relics.

The ritual will go on far after we are dead: we have nah-ting to worry about because in our family, we are *so* stubborn: whether we like it or not, we do the dance and somedays, we even love ourselves. I am really happy to say also that my contribution to the dance is fun—or fury.

I force us to joke more—that way we can stand ourselves waiting for the next laugh.
However, what I accomplished in the past and still may conduct
is a little Too deep probing of any situation.

Like I don't know how the rules went
like I had no respect or at least fear
or at least smarts
to Pretend I am dumb.

## Mama Mia's Driving

Man can that woman drive! The other day, I made up a story that when I go home, I either walk or catch the Bus because my feet are the umbilical cord attached to the *piko*, the earth. Poetic, eh? So, while walking up to the university to drop off some stuff for Victor, da Summah Skool Dean,

I noticed the weeds of my childhood along the way. I was at home being a barefoot baby in my head. I was playing with those weeds and I was talking to them as usual then I shouted silently in my adult voice, "I love to walk because then you can see stuff." No sooner had I realized this when it occurred to me that in seeing so much, I might even "see" my mother when just what? whrrr-wwhhhrrrr-whhrred pulled into view but eight tiny cylinders with a serious driver bent-backed and ferociously steering the spacecar on course: Mildred chauffeuring the Princess Marjorie en route to the eye doctor.

Did I dare flag them down and be faced with possible fire thrown against me from across the street?

What if Mildred were to be frightened into a car accident?

"Daughter kills mother by trying to say Hello?"

And what about Aunty Marjorie, the perfect human on earth?

What would she think of this "public" behavior?

And how would Mildred benefit from this—or not?

Well, I waved followed by a salute and my mother gave me the "hi" sign. After she pushed onward, the guys in the truck behind her waved to me and notably older as I am, I took this as dare <u>and</u> a threat to my dignity but after all, this was Hawai'i. To be expected, any day; any time.


That Mildred is a dri-ver though. I mean at eighty-eight! I am so scared to be in the car with her. She does some serious moves and turns at her own speed which makes my spine contract and pulls the muscles toward the back of my neck.

I stop breathing and, most of all, I cannot tell my mother what to do. Casually, she

wonders out loud

"Are you scared to drive with me?"

"Heh, heh, am I scared?"

She should stop driving and one of the younger kids should start driving the aunties

around. She's good though: once in a great while she'll say

"What the hell, you're waiting for? I need to go."

Or today while cruising the lanes at Ala Moana—missing parking space after parking space

—she let out a "Shit"

—the first shit I have ever heard my mother say in my entire life—Over missing a parking space. I kind of looked at her during the historic moment and asked if she really said "Shit."

She continued to drive and ignore me as if I were an imbecile— like I never heard anyone say "shit" before? like I had never said it a million times? And then, we found a space and proceeded to segue into our next banter.

Why try to understand?
Why try to reason?
There is a solid system in place here at home which has no reason to change
whatsoever—at least in my mother's life. *Pau hana*

## Carolyn and the Cop

It started with my waiting and waiting and waiting for the bus starting at 6:30
am to catch the Ala Moana bus to transfer to the other bus to Pearl City. While
waiting and waiting and expecting Mildred to walk out to see if I caught the
bus (because she wanted to drive me to Ala Moana) what should re-invent itself
in front of my brown black eyes but a blue and white cop car ccrrruis-singing
by and at that very moment I flashed on HIM.
No mere mortal.
HIM: not juest a thickly padded jewel.
Not just a cop but a **legend**,
a nightmare:
the something you want to forget in your early early profoundly bad
adult life.
The cop car and the cop inside were not the archetype, but the Symbol of the
man in blue reminded me of HIm.

HOw did he—him even have access to ME?
well, heh heh, He was teaching *karate* at Summer Session
and I
was taking the very first *tai qi* class offered at the UH.
We had to share the same gym. Our side, the *tai qi* class was delicate and
*tranquile* and
their side was rough and brutish—noiseyand sexual.
Our side was advanced and intelligent
and *something* about uniforms—However, while I hate to admit it, from the
distance, I noticed this Guy, good-looking from far away, and purveyor as I
was, I
scoped him out.
I cannot remember anything precisely as what led to what,
but one day he noticed me in my extraordinary aura.

He asked me if I wanted a ride home and of course, now I would refuse, but then. Then, I had never been with a cop before and only knew them collectively as PIGS.

Locals guys are Not like cops on the mainland.

At home, we can come face to face with a cop and

not take them at all seriously. They just all look like our cousins or brothers and we just know they are juvenile delinquents.

So he gave me a ride home in his own cop car because in Hawai'i, the cops can drive their own cars on the job—or at least they used to. It was blue. It was a sedan. We were both sweating from the humidity. We were both young and both cocky. I'd like to remember if we went for a ride before he brought me home or what. I remember we went to Nu'uanu and I let him know I was the sexually advanced type. He was cute.

He was as cute as all the Hawaiian boys I ever saw.

Hawaiian guys are so incredibly good-looking.

Young Hawaiian guys, old Hawaiian guys are so wild, so naughty, so so good-looking. And they are horrible—worst than Chinese because they are so good-looking and because they are so phy-phy-physical, it is such a goddamn downer when you discover they are so royaLly stupid—not no brains—that they impulsively do something stupid Because:

*It* Was Good Fun at the Moment.

That was Bumpy who smelled good and felt thck and young in my hands. That was

Bumpy who was so strong and is probably dead by now.

When it came to fucking me, it was no french movie. He just pulled and down came my panties at Kuli'ou'ou. Crushed and pounded, the taro roots became the milk and *poi* quiche—served which managed to come together *somehow*.

There was no conversation.

The ocean's voice stirred in and out.

The palm fronds wondered.

He was a cop and I was a writer but we were both Hawaiian and he was *one guy*—besides Big Kenny that my father watched. My father addressed in orders. My father wasn't nice to any of the guys that I dated with the exception of Godwin—what a name! And one thing led to another. I had a real boyfriend for a change, not some stupid student in Creative Writing. Or some membrane in Philosophy.

Bumpy was just an ordinary Hawaiian guy who was divorced and had a kid.

He fucked me quite a bit at my parent's house when they went out. I can't believe I'm even writing about this: I really should be ashamed, but this is dime for three or four dozen stuff so people at home wouldn't even consider Telling anyone about this but there Is a connection and that is up until I remembered the legend of My Very First Hawaiian Boyfriend

I didn't even know I had one and was in the meantime dreaming about—
formatting da
buggah like he was sen-sitif
and of course good-looking and first ting, had to be smart;
and with a good sense of humor and strong and healthy so he surfed and could build house and do yard work
and was nice to all the aunties.
and went fishing with the boy cousins.
Had to be able to sing and play music
and know how to get good deals
and was so nice to me and wrote music for me
and was original and of coss, I, the Bestest, deserved him.

I forgot Bumpy because I thought I as goin to turn him on with my grass one day while my parents went *holoholo* and right away Bumpy goes to the phone and pretends to be calling the vice squad. Of coss, I don know dat and I'm already stoned.
All I saw were the headlines in the Honolulu Advertiser "***O NO ONo* GIRL Arrested fo Possession of Pakalolo at Uncle Jackie and Aunty Mildred's, 1893 Iolani Palace.**" I was sure that I had pressed my luck that time. I really expected the police truck to haul me off but no, Bumpy gives me a lecture and takes the stash. And I am left to recover from my worst challenge in life.

But a few days later, that fucker drives up like nothing happened. Like I had no memory. HE had forgotten, *mais non, pas moi merci.* He wants to visit with me and I'm like
requiring Gestalt Therapy. I don't want to see him.
My mother said I wasn't home and of course, she asked why? I made up some excuse.
And then, he drove by several times and each time when I happened to be by a window, I sunk a little lower.
Then he continued to come by and the summer was over and I ws on the plane back to the Haight.

No wonder I fell for Steve: he and Bumpy have that raw instinct that I love and that dull memory which I hate.

Their fucking style is similar too: simple, coarse, hard, and good.

(usually B+ for style, A– for orgasm, A++ for engaging my idiocy)


# The Most Beautiful Sound I evah Heard—(Cuzen) aahAnnehette

> May 1, 1996
> in honor of Rose Machado's one-hundred-and twenty-fourth birthday

**When I wass a kid while learning phonics,** there was a list of words. It was the Spalding method. How would you know what "Spalding" means. But to us-es in Honolulu, Spalding = Dole pineapple, one of the main families that controlled life. What was important about the Spalding method? well, yours truly was a recipient of the missionary method of learning how to spell. One hot day in school, we had to copy a list of words in our books and we had to MEMORIZE the list. You know, I cannot memorize for nathting so youknow I had Trouble wih ds list. But memorize it, id did, and now I can teach you someting. The vertical list included

neither
foreign
sovereign
seized
(the) counterfeit
(and) forfeited
leisure

This list was a secret code of the spelling part of phonics. By memorizing this list, you were entitled to know the "i" before "e" except after "c" rule. Overly confident—private school eh—I followed this list as a footnote to the Spalding methods, ssooOOO I'd love to comment upon the list. **My** revision is as follows: neither foreign sovereign seized (the) counterfeit (and) forfeited leisure . . . weird!

Neither you know or not: *pau* . . . heh heh.

<u>Foreign</u> is everything/everybody everysound everymovement everysmell out-side my body.

<u>Sovereign</u> (aye how many know what it is tobe or not to be experiencing sovereign(ty)?

Carolyn is (ssSSS) **S**<u>eized</u> by words language(s) tones rhythms, questions.

You heard about "faking orgasm"—how's about "<u>counterfeit</u> orgasm"? can you go jail for dis?

Itched by curiosity, *Ono Ono* girl <u>forfeit</u>ed what by chasing Adventure?

<u>Leisure</u>—a richman's word. Poor folks don't know what it is to experience this word. Perhaps Richman can provide opportunities fo poo folks to feel <u>leisure</u>. And tofeel <u>leisure</u>, you cannot feel leisha for only 10 minutes oneday. You gotta know it in the blood—in Richman's family and generations to feel and ensure you can feel it again an again becuss I heard it feels so good and to feel so good, you gotta have the money thing under Kontrol. Got to. Money, lots of it—all kind style. Aye, dat's it, money: means <u>leisure</u>.

<u>Weird</u> is a itchy or scratchy feeling in the body that when it finally hits the brain, the body goes off its natural course of sleeping and eating and going to the bathroom at the right places at the right time. A longtime of <u>weird</u> will send you to Kaneohe or Napa. Or maybe you could write or dream or exercise or deny out the itchies until you feel Gooood again.

When I started writing this, I was receiving the effects of a friend's jealousy. No way was it possible for me to imagine that she could do this, but she did. Man, was like da lava and gasses and steam and tidalwave and hurricane in and around me. Good thing I like to And can laugh because the buggah was big. And it was my Kaleponi *'ohana* who wuz here for me. An after time passes, the *kupuna* and *'ohana* may even refer to dat person—as "poor ting"—but now, they have advised to me *'oki* the relationship.

WHAHT happened?
Oh daddy! I COUld say A-lot more about it, but somebody's jealousy—*lili*—became the genesis for me to investigate my genealogy. Meanwhile, it is so amazing that never in my life did I ever expect to use the word "sovereignty" like it is part of my working vocabulary which it has *Become*. And can you believe I got rhythm, I got genealogy: let me tell it, sistah. Aye, braahhh, I been wit da Mormons. From the Chinese 'mericans to the Chinese in China to the Hahawhyans to the *na o iwi Kanaka*, to the Native Americans—all different tribes, now da Mormons.

But **gotta skip to da good paht.** As I was in their "Family Center," I could only hear Steve Young's voice saying how (yes) he does wear daht long undawear. and It was such a hot day with me in shorts and sleeveless yet! and Me da only nonwhite and bang! I was home in the Territory of Hawaii real quick. and How the lady touched my hair and said I had it all mousssed and cute. All retirees. Fuck'n state of d' art technology and lots of archival stuff. No can take pen inside; no purses. Everybody fat and friendly. (an) All I could see was us hiding from da white guys in short sleeves with hats who would be ever so polite when they came to our door and talked about Jesus and stayed and stayed and stayed and smiled anticipating to be invited for a meal. Argh! Maybe I should try "visit" Steve Young as part of my missionary work as an animist and see if he invites me for dinner or lunch or More.

What did I accomplish? I sent for tūtū's death and birth certificates as well as the death certificates of her parents. (One of my Hawaiian cousins must know something.) Now I gotta write Emela and tell her what happened. Emi is my first cousin. I asked her father, Uncle Walter, my daddy's brother, "What was tūtū's real name?" because in Hawai'i, we are given so many goofy and silly names.

Uncle Walter said, "Ah dunno."

My *haole* and *pake* mind weighed his response in disbelief and only when I told da story to Yolanda it was clarified with her comment spoken in the heat one evening.

"That's not unusual. The boys don't know nothing—it's the women." Meaning that the boys are left alone to fish or surf or chase *wahine* or paddle or, or, or (*ka mea, ka mea, ka mea*).

The night I was returning to San Francisco, Emi was busy writing down the names and dates of birth for the brothers and sisters of *k'ou tūtū*, Rose Machado, who was a May Day princess born on May 1, 1872. But Emela never write down da names of da fahdda and maddah! Hhoh, I must have some special blood to have grandma but no need great grand Anything. My poor beautiful grandmother—I have two beautiful grandmothers, both make you lose your breath while you falling down because they so classy—both died not speaking a word of English. My father refused to allow his Hawaiian heritage to influence me. My mother wanted me to speak with no accent. Funny kine huh? even though now that I feel I can be who I am, until I get the birth and death records, I presume *there will be* **Those** who will still question my me-ness. I cannot help if I no have the anthropological physical NORMS of whatever Hawaiian or Chinese norm is supposed to be by whoever is judging at the moment. So much for **multicultural** (wo)man who want live without justafying justiifying justifying all time this or that.

### K'ou *Untitled* 'Ohana
### *My (as of yet) Unnamed Family*

I called Owana about this—actually, I woke her up. She was really nice and understanding. It was the best person that I could have spoken to because she is my cousin and she understood. The <u>weird</u> part was the public position of the family's profile. That was so <u>weird</u>—that the family—really her side has inherited some powaful *mana* in "what we can offer." That was so <u>weird</u> to speak in third person. However, she did have solid advice which she shared with me "cuz to cuz"—and at another level, *ali'i nui* to *maka'āinana* (highest monarch to worker). Her voice was warm and I could feel her thinking as she spoke.

"Just be *nanea*"    *she sang in her voice like sunset*
"reeelax, have a good time in the meantime.
The Time will come
and you'll **k**now

exactly what to do and how to respond to this person.

If you plan now, all the factors may be different, when the moment arrives."

my cousin **smart, eh ?** so gifted in giving advice.

That was right. I felt her being—which is so different from the Chinese—or all of Asia for that matter. (Critics! have a blast: document, prepare. attack) God bless them but they have little or no experience with Solving—really confronting and solving emotions like sadness and disappointment. New shoes, a good meal, an outing has always been the quick fix for the mighty A:S(iN) way: it's like they are too scared, too busy, or simply uninterested in why a person could be hurt. (generally) They are sour having been educated through the mighty an(si/ci)[e]ant (you are not humord to witness and errow on the menue "of some Asianne restaurant" an arrow in spelLing?) Soapopery and I dunno.
The Confusciant slaves tend to scowl or lecture if a person is down so I never told "the Ai-[xin] (trans. "love" "heart") community" when this matter happened. Lost Souls, the confusciants lack humor—the worst.

The lesson would go something like
"That's what you get from straying from our ways or living so far away."

Nem-mind, nemmine soon I'll see Emi and the other cousins.

I should have realized to tell them sooner. They would have *mālama* immediately, but I have learned the meaning of the word *lili* in the meantime.


## *Kaleponi* 'Ohana

And the hurt still continues but the healing goes on. Yesterday, I received a very sweet card from the Kaleponi *'ohana*. Cliff and Earl sent it but I received the message from the entire *'ohana*.

> Dear Carolyn—We missed you at the get together on Saturday. All our thoughts went out to you.
> We hope you will feel the *'ohana* is here for you. We will ride this out with you. You are not alone.

All our love & *aloha*,

*'Ohana o ka hale wai aloha o ka wai puna o kane*

When Yolanda came over today to practice my *ONO ONO GIRL* signature song *Kai Mana Hila* so that I can dance it all by myself, we took a moment to *wala 'au* the whole thing all over again. *Kūkā Kūkā* it was. Back and forth, forth and back, weaving until it got a little deeper and I began to see just how much the *'ohana* accepts me just the way I am. And I'm thinking how not unusual I am in that there are more babies being born of mixed-race parentage, and the optimistic line that "We take from the good and leave the bad behind." How life works, however! Sometimes, Who and What determines what is Good and Bad are beyond one's control. Too much *aloha* can be dangerous, but how could I not be like that? I AM too much *aloha* if *aloha* can be too much. I like being nice to people.
In the old days, if someone was not *pono*, they got slap on the head or I dunno. Now, we just remember *that* family name. Yes.

### June 18, 1996, and Who was Julia Edward(s)?

I've been talking to my cousin Annette for the last several days and I am in love. I adore my cousin Annette Neuhause or maybe Annette Newhouse whom I met for the first time in my life on Tuesday, June 18, 1996, at the armory where our cousin Kalanihiapo had hidden to defend Liliu'okalani (really Owana's cousin, though our very gorgeous cousin Helen de Rego received an invitation to the ceremonies for the statue's unveiling—see page 72).

Annette and I were outside our bodies as we anticipated meeting each other and slipped right back as we spotted each other and waved. We changed our unnamed 'ohana prayer which we name as Laughing and Kissing And Studying, Talking and Laughing and Travelling.

We wasted no time crying in the classic way of most 'ohana: we had work to do. We had waited and waited and dreamed and hoped and waited so graciously and patiently too many years for each other. We had no time to live up to the standards of classic anything.

After we hugged and kissed, I ran over to the Parking Guy about to collect revenue for the city and asked if he would take our picture. He obliged while we posed for history.

Then we went straight to work at the old archives—which is quite beautiful. I asked the receptionist if we could meet in the conference room and I think she thought I was *maha'oi* but I didn't care—it belongs to history and we in the process of creating some. Then I sweetly asked if I could turn on the lights— *nui po'e haole nani*, beautiful—and she suspiciously inquired how long we were going to be? Whatever I said, she let us turn on the lights and my darling cousin and I proceeded to share our *ukana* of family faces with each other. Annette hauled out a gigantic portrait the size of a hat box of her grandmother Mary; and I took out my small chapbook which I hate but has a photo of daddy and *tūtū* and *tūtū* man on the cover. She showed me photos of her *mo'opuna* who are now part of me and I part of them. The moment was volcanic with emotion. On the wall, the full-sized oil portraits of Kawananakoa groaned with envy. From Kaka'ako to 'Iolani Palace, my new cousin and I were silent with happiness.

Then we walked to the new archives, which is right behind the old archives— heh, even archives can be old, older—and where would the oldest archives be I wonder? So we *hele* on. uuUUh so interesting in that place. No pens, no purses again. And pictures of the young Japanese prince (who was supposed to be engaged to Princess Ka'iulani) and I said, "Aye, he look just like one gang member, eh?" and we giggled.

When we got into "The Room," we were even more excited but our excitement was put on hold by our new boyfren (a kind of frog prince). LIvely Mr. Espinda held us at tongue-point and nice-girls us, listened. On and On Mr. Espinda chanted his genealogy Portagee style while Annette and I glanced at each other and tried to slip away. But politician, storyteller, and *kupuna* that he was, Mr. Espinda shared his glorious family history with us.

When we finally escaped Mr. Espinda, Annette and I began to investigate. Oh, we were so excited and Annette is such a darling. You would fall in love with my cousin. Not somebody on tv. No movie star. No director: a true scholar, and that's how it really should be done because one of the reasons why Annette is so eager about everything is that she tells and shows her *mo'opuna* (gran babies) all the lovely things they should be knowing. She takes them on the free electric bus to show them old Hawai'i, she is realllllly special and she is My partner in this genealogy project.

Aye, an by da way, dis genealogy stuff, *nui pilikia*, real trouble. So stupid to try to get anSas from the archives. Sooooo *kapulu*. Da people work dere—most dem: sa-wa pusses. An No help, nahting. Get one fat japannee lady do nahting but only say

"We do not interpret," and smile.

Whoa! and da kind drawer you see that the libray-ree—da wooden drawer, only get pieces of cut-up white recycled paper with handwritten in pen or pencil statistics. Sta-tistics, man! And no mo da long pin down in the bottom with the *puka* to hold da buggah so da stuff no can fall out from da drawer!

no mo da *puka*, no mo da pin. How? you like dat!

Anybody can sign Anyyteeng.
Can make graffiti if I like.
Can erase or add on.
First name I saw in the "M" section. Boom: "illigitimate" right under da name.
Aye? how come *nui po'o haole*?
Shame, eh?

Man, I wanted to trow dat drawer on da floor and mess da whole thing up.
Dass not Hawaiian.

I wass burned up.
I went *niele* the *buke*.
Nice thing about doing genealogy is that you never know what nice kind people
you goine meet like the nice ladies who waved to us as they drove off singing
"Good-bye cousins," because Annette and I were wearing our *pakalana* lei.
Nice to meet Hawaiians in the archives. Everybody looking up something. so
cute.

How come I got the *palapala*—the original documents and Annette was forced
to research the microfilm? "Ah dunno"
but we were excited by seeing the actual documents of our big *tūtū* or *tūtū
tūtū* TOOtoo who was not only married twice which we already knew aBout
but married maybe three times and was in San Francisco in 1902 when my
*tūtū* was getting married to daddy's daddy. The name "Keola" came up—tūtū's
first husband and when we talked to Emi later, we wondered just how many
children *tūtū* had because Emi's father's birth certificate indicated that *tūtū* had
more children then we could account for from our *tūtū* man. We also know
that there isss a lot of confusing signals (words) on those papers: the dates and
ages never match. (what are the general consequences?) We still cannot find the
Hawaiian strain of the genealogy because in our family we marry and adopt a
lot—common for many Hawaiian families also. We are lots and lots and lots of
cousins and at least for now, we cannot chant the family history—but Annette
and I and all the cousins are planting and sweating and laughing and making
babies and dancing and changing the everlasting changing rhythm of the *'ohana*.
And we are very happy.
We love to be with each other laughing and kissing, talking deep story, talking
history laughing and laughing even when we cry
we could ease in a laugh because we love to feel happy so much.
Which is getting tougher and tougher to say about most folks.

When I last saw Annette, we were supposed to search the birth records that
day but I was so concerned that my ballot for the Native Hawaiian vote had not
been received (typical: I made sure that my kids' were all in order but I Forgot
to sign and date MINE!). So We jamboreeed to the palace where we inquired if
there were any election applications. The *kupuna* there motioned us on to OHA
(Office of Hawaiian Affairs) where we could probably find some. Annette said,

"Aye we can do our genealogy any day. It's here forever. Would you like to register?"

The magic words. Yes, I wanted to be SURE that I was registered.

We smiled while the lovely lady took our picture and we walked on—past Honolulu *Hale* stopping at the Mission Houses (which was <u>weird</u>). We walked on through the KSBE (Kamehemeha Schools/Bishop Estate) compound. We crossed the street and the parking attendant directed us to OHA, which was in the big building down the street. At OHA, I reapplied to vote, then it was down the elevator onto Kaka'ako where Annette grew up and where my daddy used to live. Through the heat we yakked pausing briefly at the old GEM where I ate a Vietnamese sandwich and Annette told more stories. We continued past Ward Warehouse (mall) and now we were in shape: we could have walked to Leahi but stopped at Ala Moana where we would catch our separate buses.

When we got to Ala Moana (the mall of course), I remembered that I forgot to bring the James Dean stamps that I had bought to give Annette. When I said this to my cousin, she jumped out of her body.

All her emotion focused in her eyes and mouth shaped like a double rainbow zipping off into a star over the waterfalls, *ohia*, all the royal family of flowers and their attendants: Annette had that look.

We were in the image of the card that I had given her: we were on our horses in the *kuahiwi*. Cousins!

Annette was a young barefoot girl with bean bags in her hands

The pistil from a red hibiscus sprung from her nose

Mynah birds were walking and squawking

Her feet were diving in the sky

We are the *'ohana* from the void: we are the leaders from beyond.

Our mission statement is "Don't follow us"

My cousin was happy and I could be so happy as we hugged each other in the midst of cars and noise and heat and sweat. Of couse dat was the moment.

When I came back to Oakland, I didn't want to write her because I really want to hear the red dirt and the multiple orgasm chocolate cake and her smile and the waves of laughter in her voice and the way she turns her head slightly while she is poised to say her *mana'o*.

Instead, Annette in her beautiful handwriting wrote

"Dear *Ono Ono* Girl" as her first words and proceeded to tell me that she hadn't returned to the archives because now the *mo'opuna* are there more often. And after 5 pm, I called her the very day I received that post card in honor of the last day to register to vote.

## What now?

I talked to Eirelan today and she returned her ballot while I still have not yet received mine.

Ana is in Costa Rica watching the turtles lay eggs to the tune of parrots and monkeys.

Almost everyone I know who can, will be voting.

My mother is doing better with the goal of Las Vegas in the future.

And of course I will go home to torment my mother in the grand tradition that I tormented my mother's mother who loved me dearly—you think she goine like it?

Steve is fine. Steve *si* godd: I have convinced him that he and Scottie Pippin—my real love—look alike. I will now try to convince Steve that
Steve looks like Matthew McConaughey

I will see Milton and Thomas today—a double-hitter literary scene; two cultures and languages leagues away but *intime* nonetheless.

I'm in love—with Me ov coss
The rest of the world is watching the glad-i-gator spectacle, the abuse of humans also known as the olympics while I danced the best ballet class

The weather is good
I got my ballot. Voted. Took a picture of my ballot and sent it right back
*I mua!*

# 6

## *Ho'okolohe*

*heh heh*


## Blistering, Baalassting Off with My Buddies: Smiling

Christmas Day, I got the fax: **Kasumi PASSSED THE LAST EXAM FOR POTENTIAL ASTRONATUS!**

**Dear Spottie Dottie, she wrote and**
thanked me for the artistic letter and book. She read my letter "loudly" when she was alone at home. She especially liked the part about me "barking" (which I did not do, I "screamed") at the Kinokuniya. She liked the poem I wrote based upon *Woman in the Dunes*, whose central character I refer to as "Kasumi" who becomes Woman of the Pine Needles who climaxes to be Woman of the Apples who births and nourishes herself—though Hello (Kitty) herself was still trying to understand the meaning and, at the time, had not read my essay "*Almost a Man*"—which I sure will give her Pa-lenty to think about as most English speakers don't get the point of the essay.

She went on to tell me her great news, believing it was because she selected the right answers for 19th-Century French Art and 8th-Century Japanese Buddhism Art in the general education part of the exam, although she couldn't solve the problems about pulleys in the physics section. And much like Hello Kitty, she wondered why there were no questions on music!? There will be more tests and I meanwhile am praying that my friend will be selected. In the last paragraph of her letter she charmingly writes

> I think I would be OK for athletic tests and interviews but not sure about the detailed medical exams. I might have a strange waveform in the brain or in the heart as like only the people from Mars have. Lets see what happens next.

and when she visited me, Kasumi told me that in Japan(ese), we "don't need Subject." Okay

**Let's see what happens next.** *A hui hou kākou*

## *ONO ONO* GIRL FAN CLUB

### ELIGIBILITY REQUIREMENTS
1. **Extremely emotional**
2. **Uncontrollable sex drive**
3. **Good-sounding laughter**
4. **Loves to sing**
5. **Loves to dance**
6. **Can tell Funny stories**
7. **Hates teachers**
8. **Hates an "impeccable" house**
9. **Needs regular orgasm**
10. **Adores extended foreplay**
11. **Loves to waste time**
12. **Will not hesitate beating anybody up through teasing**
13. **Does not speak good English**
14. **Is somewhat vain**
15. **Profoundly insecure**
16. **Hates lawyers**
17. **Worships sharks, owls, rocks, lizards**
18. **Refuses to be trained**

EXTRA POINTS:
19. **Worked in the pineapple cannery**
20. **Can climb trees**
21. **Got cracks in the feet from a barefooted child and adult life**
22. **Got no future**


## *ONO ONO* Inner Snacktum

**To succeed from the Fan Club to the Inner Snacktum, an application is provided. Please respond to the following items in the narrative.**

I. What do you envision as your personal *ONO ONO* immediate goals? the long-term goals?                                         (10 pts)

II. How do you feel about bad breath?
    What do you believe is the cause?
    Do you have any prescription for BB?                          (5pts)

III. How would you shift a boring tale into a lively one?          (40 pts)

IV. Imagine *ONO ONO* Volcanic National Park. Security gates surround the Park, a virtual *ahupua'a* (ecosystem) with no money exchanged within the gates. All visitors would contribute to the *ahupua'a* by doing manual labor (aka yardwork). Everybody—no excuses—works because good work is good fun.
    1. What cottage industries do you perceive as a result?
    2. Describe the infrastructure.
    3. What language(s) would be spoken?                          (15 pts)

V. Do you believe in *'aumakua*?
    1. Translate *'aumakua* into English? Chinese? Spanish? Sioux? Swahili? Tagalog? French? German? Greek? Yiddish? Italian? Inuit? Pakistani? Japanese? Portuguese? Vietnamese? Maidu?                    (30 pts)

                                                    Total    100 pts

## *Hana Hou* (more NOW)

Aunty Bea said now I'm "graduate" of her and Aunty Kika.
I said, "Oh, I'm *alaka'i!*"

Jacqueline and I are happy.

Thank you daddy for sending me life—what powa(s) you got!

I do miss my Popo and Tai Yi. *Mahalo tūtū* and *tūtū* man and all the *'ohana*

And now, we all chant from the *ONO ONO* GIRL mission statement:

"I want to be healthy, pay my bills, and not be grouchy"

Sending all the bestest love and fun happinesses

ahHnnnn here comes some     sweet

wet *ono ono* kisssses

**I love you.**

**OOG**